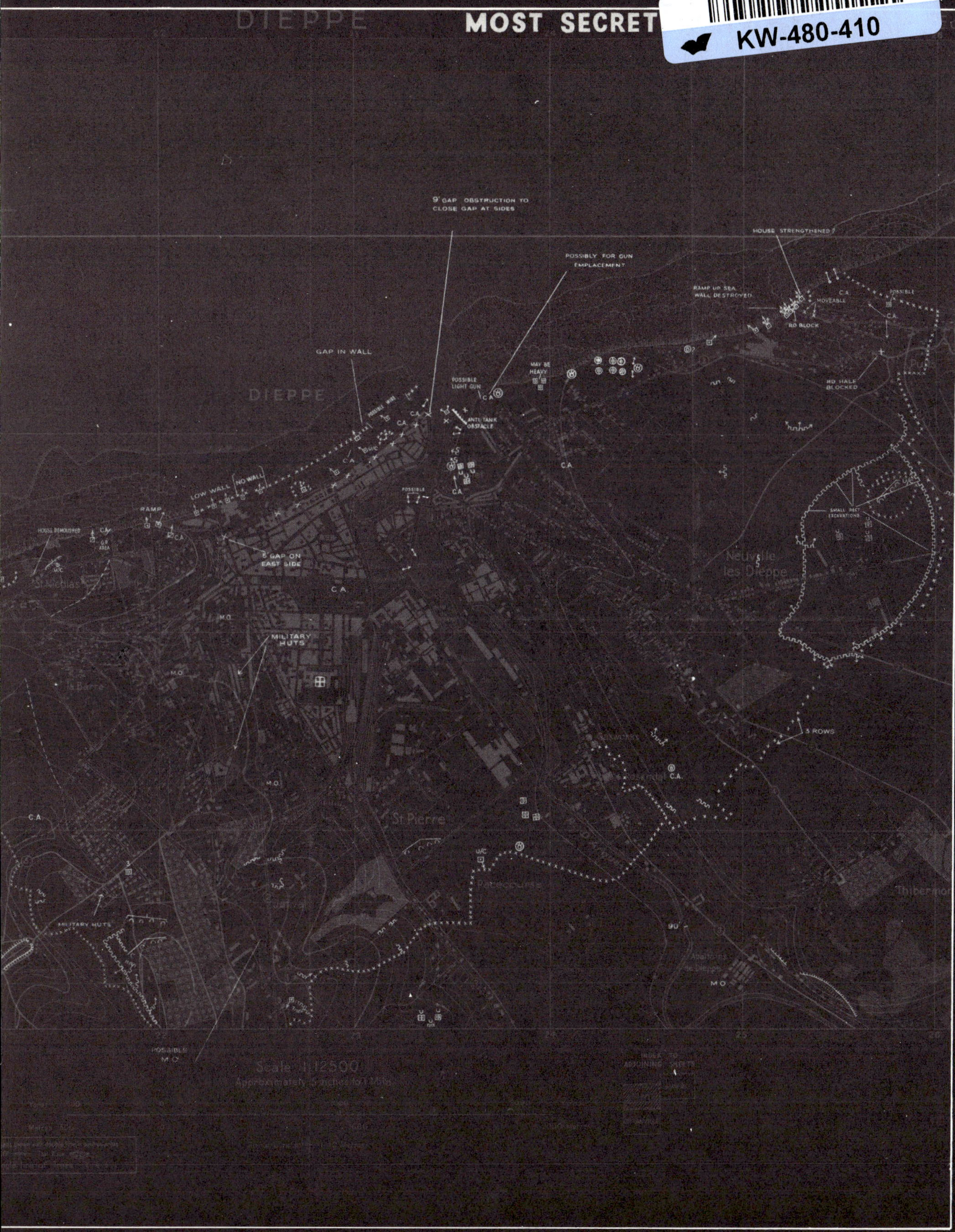

DIEPPE

MOST SECRET

9' GAP OBSTRUCTION TO CLOSE GAP AT SIDES

HOUSE STRENGTHENED ?

POSSIBLY FOR GUN EMPLACEMENT

RAMP UP SEA WALL DESTROYED

C.A. MOVEABLE

POSSIBLE C.A.

RD BLOCK

GAP IN WALL

MAY BE HEAVY

POSSIBLE LIGHT GUN

RD HALF BLOCKED

DIEPPE

ANTI TANK OBSTACLE

LOW WALL

NO WALL

RAMP

HOUSE DEMOLISHED

C.A.

SMALL RECT EXCAVATIONS

5' GAP ON EAST SIDE

Neuville les Dieppe

M.O.

MILITARY HUTS

3 ROWS

St Pierre

MILITARY HUTS

POSSIBLE M.O.

Scale 1:12500

Vue sur le Casino (R. Jourde, Arch.) et la Plage.
335 DIEPPE

Introduction

In the earliest morning hours of August 19, 1942, an armada of almost 250 Allied vessels left southern England, carrying over 6,000 troops and sixty tanks towards a dawn assault on the German-occupied port of Dieppe, just across the English Channel. Seventy squadrons of fighters and bombers, flown by pilots of eight nations, provided air cover for this reconnaissance-in-force whose mission was to occupy Dieppe and hold it for a matter of hours before withdrawing.

Ever since, the questions have gone on. How did such a massive, short-lived operation come about, what did it accomplish and why was it such a bitter, costly failure?

The force consisted of several hundred British commandos and marines, 50 U.S. Rangers, some two dozen Free French commandos. . .and almost 5,000 Canadian soldiers. German casualties were less than 600; Allied casualties were almost 4,000.

Among the Canadians killed, wounded or taken prisoner were the following: out of 554 of Toronto's Royal Regiment of Canada—524; out of 582 of the Royal Hamilton Light Infantry—480; out of 553 of Windsor's Essex Scottish—530; out of 584 of Quebec's Fusiliers Mont-Royal—513; out of 503 of the Queen's Own Cameron Highlanders from Winnipeg—

346; out of 523 of the South Saskatchewan Regiment—339; and out of 417 of the Fourteenth Canadian Army Tank Regiment (the Calgary Tanks)—174.

It is small wonder that the very word *Dieppe* chills the hearts of an entire generation of Canadians.

What follows may not add a great deal of historical fact to the excellent accounts that have been written about the raid, nor provide any new answers to the questions that have raged around its disasters. This is less a history than an impression based on the memories of those who took part in

the battle. Whatever resentments they have expressed are seldom directed against individuals who may be named in the history books, but rather against the anonymous "them" who make up any bureaucracy—be it military, political or commercial.

Perhaps, if blame is to be assigned, it must be shared by everyone involved in the raid on Dieppe—by those who planned it, for their mistakes; by those who fought in it, for their inexperience; and by those who wanted it in the first place, for their inability to resist playing the military and political game of war.

ECHOES OF DISASTER

DIEPPE 1942

First published in Great Britain 1982 by

Richard Drew Publishing Limited
20 Park Circus
Glasgow G3 6BE
Scotland

ISBN 0 86267 006 3

Printed and bound in Canada

The publisher has made every effort to give accurate credit to the sources of quotations and illustrations which appear in this book. In the event of error or omission, notification would be appreciated.

Acknowledgments

The author's special thanks are due to Terence Macartney-Filgate, the book's editor and the producer-director of the two Canadian Broadcasting Corporation television films on which the book is based. His meticulous research, unflagging enthusiasm and sympathetic interviews with over 200 survivors of the Dieppe raid have made possible both this book and the two films. A debt of deep gratitude is also owed to Jennifer Hodge for her cheerful encouragement and for conducting the German and French interviews; to Tom Berner, the film editor of the television specials, for his discerning eye in assessing photographs and drawings; to all those who loaned photographs and drawings, many of them treasured personal mementos; to all those whose memories are quoted herein; and to five Dieppe veterans whose company during a visit to Dieppe taught the author a lesson in courage, and made him thankful that it could be learned on a battlefield decades after the battle. The five are Ed Bennett, Harry Long, Con Stapleton, Lucien Dumais and the colonel of the F.M.R. at Dieppe, Dollard Menard.

For those who died young in war that we may grow old in peace and for Tiff.

August 19 1942

The beach at Dieppe August 19, 1942

By late afternoon the beach at Dieppe was littered with the debris of battle. Headlines in Canada, Britain and the United States would soon be trumpeting a mighty victory, but for the survivors of 5,000 young Canadians who embarked on the Dieppe raid, the name of this French resort on the Channel coast of Normandy would forever ring with the bitterness of defeat.

The echoes of this disaster can still be heard.

The cost of military and political folly was horrendous . . .

Every tank that landed had to be sacrificed. Thirty-three landing-craft were stranded on the beach. Out of a total force of 6,000 men—most of them Canadian—the wounded, dead and prisoners of war added up to more than 3,600.

Dieppe, August 19, 1942

. . .and the objective was impossible.

How could any landing force succeed in crossing this expanse of open beach in daylight—with a murderous cross-fire coming down from the cliffs at either end and a rain of bullets pouring from buildings all along the front?

View from west headland, Dieppe, August 19, 1942

Not a single tank and only a handful of men managed to get into the town.

West headland and beach at Dieppe, August 19, 1942

Dieppe, August 19, 1942

Dieppe, August 19, 1942

The sea wall, Dieppe, August 19, 1942

Dieppe, August 19, 1942

For most, the war ended right here.

Nineteen hundred Canadians were marched off into German prison camps.

The captured survivors of the Dieppe raid now had the rest of the war to reflect on their only taste of battle. For most, Dieppe was their first—and last—experience with the realities of warfare. It was a bitter lesson in which German casualties were less than 600, while Allied casualties totalled almost 4,000.

Canadians surrender in Dieppe, August 19, 1942

What had the sacrifice gained?

Canadian dead, Dieppe, August 19, 1942

How did such a disaster come about?

Canadian prisoners of war, Dieppe, August 19, 1942

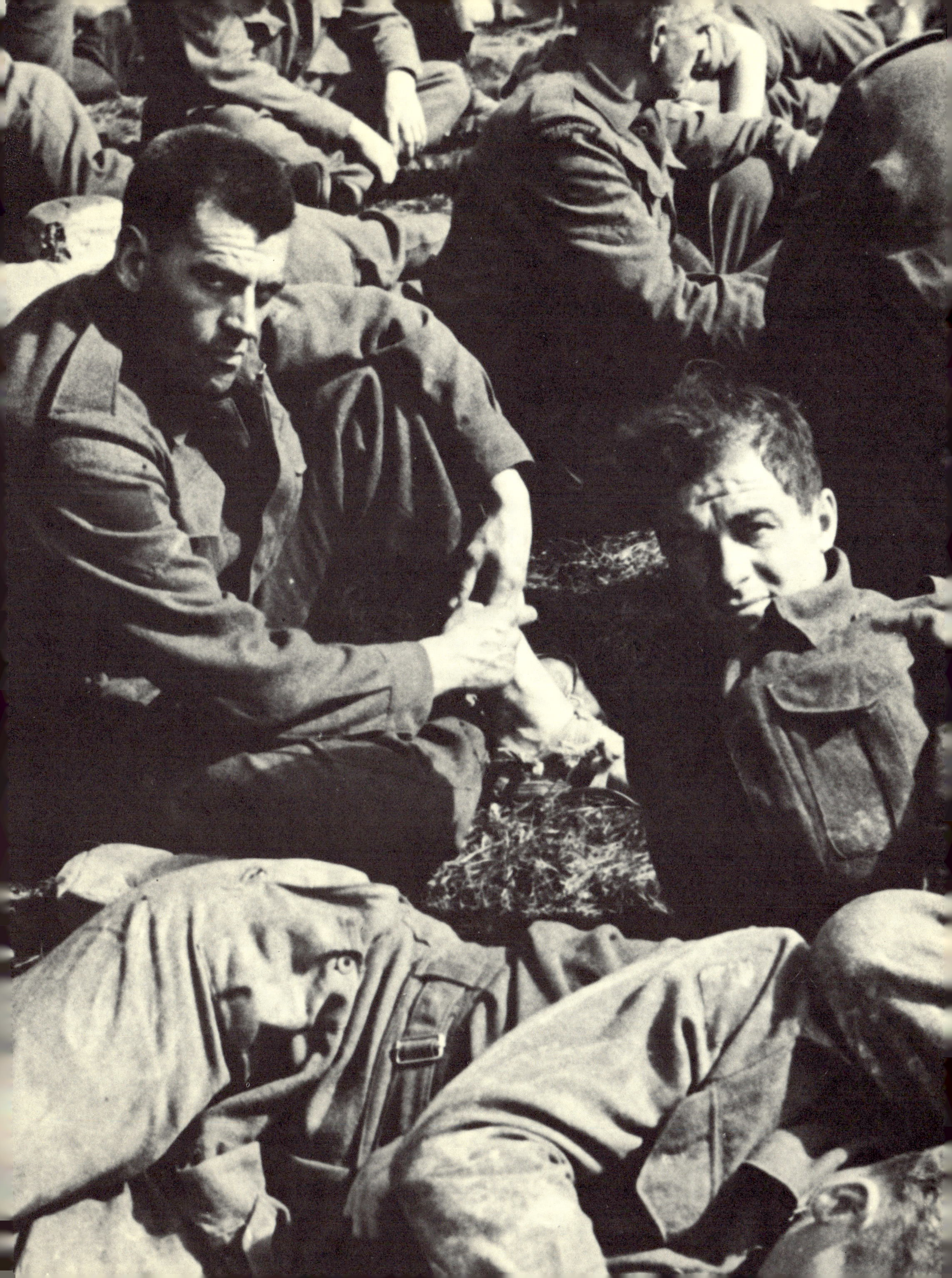

September 10 1939

...picked up in the ...night following the torpedo...

...The submarine was believed sunk later by ...which dropped depth bombs. This picture was flown ...by clipper and sent to Toronto by wirephoto. The girls are Rowena Simpson, Maxine Robinson, Betty Stewart...

TROLLEYS FORM BARRICADES FOR DEFENDERS OF WARSAW

Women and Children Help Dig Trenches as Bombs Fall—Shops Open

LONG SIEGE AHEAD

Budapest, Sept. 11—Warsaw dug in for its fourth day of siege today. The German attacking force launched more than 40 air raids and ...untless tank attacks yesterday. ...Lwow, 210 miles to the south...st and capital of the Polish Ukraine, the radio instructed the city's defenders to dig trenches and ...ct street barricades.

...ere were indications the German drive already had started. Throughout the broadcast from Lwow, sirens could be heard sounding air raid alarms.

It appeared Lwow, one of the chief industrial centres in southeastern Poland, was to be subjected to the same sort of battering that has taken place at the gates of Warsaw since the German forces reached there last Friday.

While general headquarters of the Polish army, in a broadcast from Lwow, insisted "Warsaw is ready for a long defence" and stressed that action on the Franco-German front" has now really started," the government broadcasting station at Warsaw also issued a warning of the impending attack on Lwow.

Women and Children Help

To the accompaniment of air raid ...rens and motors of diving planes, ...e Warsaw announcer said civil...ns in both cities were helping in ...fence, with aged men and women ...d children doing whatever they ...ld.

...arly this morning, Polish Staff ...tain Vaclav Pilinski, in a broad... from the capital, said Polish

(Continued on Page 3, Col. 4)

...RK MAKES VISI...

FRANCO PRESERVING STRICT NEUTRALITY

Orders Germans Away From Spanish-French Border

Paris, Sept. 11—(UP)—General Francisco Franco, Spanish nationalist leader, is ordering all German civilians, including mining engineers, to withdraw from the French border zone as part of his neutrality policy, it was understood today.

Marshal Henri Petain, ambassador to Spain, was reported to have advised Foreign Minister Georges Bonnet at a conference here this morning that Gen. Franco had given him personal assurance that Spain intended to preserve strict neutality and had pledged that Spain would adopt a good neighbor policy toward France. Petain was believed to have made the same report to Premier Daladier.

GERMAN MINES SINK NAZI TORPEDO BOAT

Swedish Ship Reports 10 Dead in Blast

Copenhagen, Sept. 11—(CP)—The Copenhagen newspaper Berlingske Aftenavis reported today that a German torpedo boat exploded in a German mine field off Trelleborg, Sweden, yesterday, with an estimated loss of 10 lives.

The paper said the explosion was seen by a Swedish ship which was unable to go to the rescue because of the mines. A German trawler rescued some of the crew, the dispatch added. The master of the Swedish vessel said ...the water... ...rished in

CANADA DE... WAR FIRST IN HER H...

Week's Interval Ena... livery of Fighting ...ment From U.S.

SIGNED BY MR.

By R. W. LIPSETT

Ottawa, Sept. 11—Canada ...war with Germany. With fo... adequate to gain the appro... the most exacting propone... national sovereignty, the Dom... on Sunday issued a proclamatio... claring that a state of war e... between this country and the R...

It was another precedent in C...ada's constitutional evolution ...first time the Dominion ...declared war. Publication of ...proclamation by the King's prin... in a special edition of the offic... gazette accomplished the declar...tion, and less than an hour later th... United States proclaimed it... Neutrality Act in operation agains... Canada as an active belligerent.

Thus was brought to a conclusion a week of hectic constitutional argument as to where Canada stood technically in the matter of hostilities with Germany. From the time Britain declared war, Canada was at war and liable to attack by the enemy. But Canada was not an active belligerent in the eyes of the United States until yesterday's proclamation was issued, and during

(Continued on Page 8, Col. 6)

LIFEBOAT FIRED ON SAYS LETTER TO CITY

Mrs. H. McKillop Writes Husband About Athenia

One of the first letters reaching Toronto from an Athenia passenger came to H. McKillop, Southview Ave., today from his wife. Mrs. McKillop, her daughter, Julia, 3, and son, Harold, 10, were rescued.

Air mailed from Galway, Ireland, Sept. 7, the letter says: "We are all well here, the children just fine. They were not hurt—only little bruises.

"It was just terrible. We had only come up after having dinner when we were fired upon.

"I still don't know how I saved the children. It was the hand of God with us. We have lost everything, have no money and nothing but our lives.

"When we were in... they fired...

...10,000- ...Stun- ...ofoten, ...north- ...ship

Sew... M...

BOM...

Amste...saw was ...city alm... Polish ...needles a... genious a... their chil... and burned...

Eric Calc...pher, told ...arrived here ...—his head ...memories" o... en to...

Hungry 30's rod-riders hop train c. 1933

Line-up at soup kitchen c. 1934

city was obeying the burg... they "defend themselves to the last d... Stirred by the valiant defence of ... France were forming "a great new uni... Paris reports said the Polish force... along the middle portion of the Vistula ... said, "the situation seems less grave." An official German communique ... Nazi advance had been checked.

VALIANT RESISTANCE

Budapest, Sept. 11—(UP and AP) ... asserted today that the capital was hold... attack by German artillery and airplanes. The city withstood 14 air raids by 70 ... Sunday, it was asserted, and 15 German pl... down, including five which crashed in the ... Numerous buildings were in flames, th... as the result of hits by five German bombs. The Warsaw radio said German bombs ... Square, which is ringed by the war ministry, ... saw military headquarters and the Hotel Eu... foreigners stayed before war started. The fragmentary report, interru... number of persons were ... Two Ger...

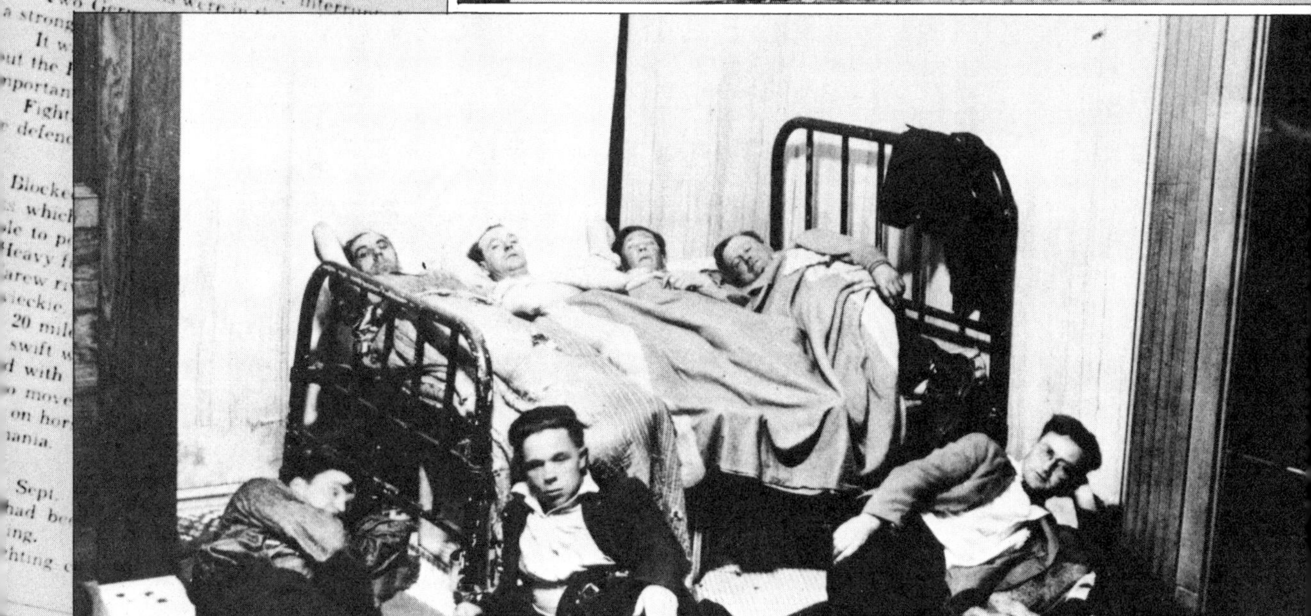

H MOTHERS TIE COTTO...
ABIES FOR GAS MAS...

Protectors Over ...arsaw Awaits ...f Poison

BRITISH PREMIER THANKS CANAD...

London, Sept. 11—Prime M... ister Chamberlain today sent ... message to Canadian Prime M... ister King, thanking him for hi... personal message announcing Canada's entry into the war. "It is a profound encourage-ment to me," wrote Chamberlain, "to know that under your leader-ship Canada has declared her in-tention to employ her great re-sources in common resistance to German aggression."

...RY HOUR

...—(UP)—War... ...re today as a ...as masks, but ...taken their ...made an in... ...the lungs of ...ing choked ... photogra... when he ...n Warsaw

THE WEA...

Canada goes to war.

The end of the Depression was in sight.

For a decade, Canada had been gripped by drought and unemployment. With the memories of the horrors and decimation of World War I fading beneath the noisy twenties and the dirty thirties, many welcomed the chance to focus on something like another war—and to begin to forget the privations of the pre-war years.

For many young men, soldiering was their first chance to earn a living.

Royal Rifles of Canada Enlistment Centre

"A lot of these boys were actually from starving families. This is one of the reasons they went into the army—to get some money, and to get another mouth less to feed. Lots of them did that."

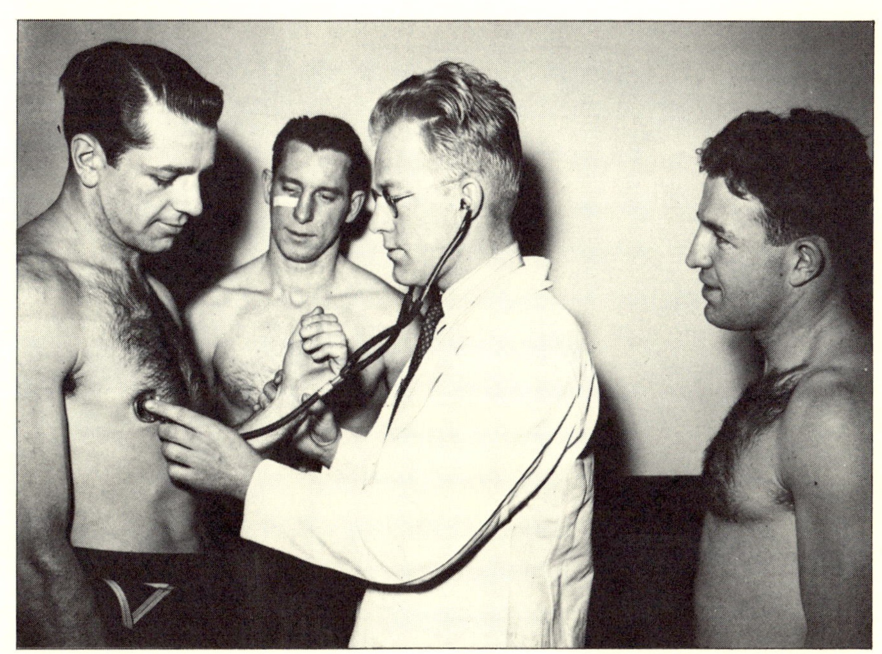

Bobby Bauer, Porky Dumart, Milt Schmidt, Boston Bruin Hockey Club front line, who left hockey to become members of the R.C.A.F., seen taking their medicals

"There were a lot of fellows that were finally getting fed every day and had some clothes to wear. I wasn't quite that bad but I was getting awful close to it in 1939."

The army began to turn farm boys . . .

Archie Anderson grew up in Alberta during the Depression, and like many young men from prairie farming communities, he knew his way around heavy machinery. This made him an excellent candidate for one of the army's mechanized regiments.

Archie Anderson

. . .into soldiers.

Archie Anderson joined the Fourteenth Canadian Army Tank Regiment—the Calgary Tanks.

Archie Anderson

Camp Borden 1940. Old Renault tanks (1920's vintage) obtained from U.S. without armament to train Canadian Tank Regiments

14th Canadian Army Tank Regiment (Calgary Tanks)

Tent towns sprang up across the country.

Army camps became communities of new recruits, but the trainees, for the most part, already knew one another. The regiments destined to fight at Dieppe each sprang from a particular part of the country. Young men who had grown up together now readied themselves to fight together.

"They came, and they came not only as individuals, they came as families. For instance, myself, my two brothers and a brother-in-law, all went in at the same time."

Camp Shilo, Manitoba

Playing-fields were taken over for war-games.

"We were all together—our age group. There were at least 150 men from my little town of 2,500. . .all in the same group and all together. We'd started together in the old reserve army and we went through together as long as we lasted."

Camp Shilo, Manitoba

Canadian recruit

"I had some serious thought about it, too. I wasn't that young—I was twenty-four years old. And I had some serious thought and I thought, this is one thing that I must do, that I really wanted to do."

Some were outfitted and trained for tropical warfare—and many would be among the casualties in the defence of Hong Kong in 1941.

Canada's Second Division arrives in Britain, December, 1940

The Second Canadian Division arrived in Britain in December, 1940.

These were the men whose fate it was to fight at Dieppe: Toronto's Royal Regiment of Canada, the Royal Hamilton Light Infantry, the Essex Scottish from Windsor, Quebec's Fusiliers Mont-Royal, the Queen's Own Cameron Highlanders from Winnipeg, the South Saskatchewan Regiment, the Calgary Tanks and Calgary Highlanders, the Toronto Scottish Regiment, the Black Watch of Canada and the supporting units of signallers, engineers and medical corps.

Training in Britain lasted so long . . .

Two Canadian divisions were held in England all through the threat of a German invasion from across the Channel. Then, when Hitler's hopes of invading Britain faded, nobody could decide what to do with all the Canadian soldiers—except to keep them training. Long route marches and field exercises became routine.

A mess hall in Britain

Training in Britain

Training in Britain, summer, 1941

Canadian soldiers on parade in Britain, winter of 1940-41

. . .Canadian troops were in danger of losing their fighting edge.

The men grew restless. . .bored. They looked for diversions, and found them on the hunting fields and with the British civilians—whose own sons, fathers, brothers and boy-friends were away fighting the war.

"What dragged the training out was that most of the fellows were becoming. . .call it 'domesticated.' They worked all day long, but they were just waiting to get off duty at night to go out with their girl-friends or down to the closest pub."

British girls and Canadian soldiers

The end of a day of shooting hares

Members of Canadian Armed Forces entertaining British audiences

The Canadian army volunteered to help with the British harvest . . .

Canadian soldiers help with British harvest, 1941

...while just across the Channel, German soldiers were helping the French.

German soldiers help with French harvest, 1941

By 1942, top-level pressures were mounting.

Prime Minister Mackenzie King had to get his troops into action.

After over a year of inactivity in Britain, Canadian soldiers were pressing to get into the fight—and their families back home were beginning to join in the protest. Public dissatisfaction could mean a loss of votes.

Addressing 10,000 troops assembled for track and field meet. Gen. McNaughton behind

Stalin and Roosevelt began to call for a second front.

With German forces invading Russia, and the United States eager to join the European fighting, England was receiving calls to launch a joint assault that would take the pressure off the Russians. . .just at a time when Churchill had neither the men nor the means to mount the kind of operation that was needed.

Joseph Stalin

Walking between lines of Canadian bayonets Mackenzie King inspects the guard of honour provided by the Regiment de la Chaudiere

CANADA

Left to right: Prime Minister Winston Churchill, President Roosevelt and Prime Minister W.L. Mackenzie King, 1943

Churchill was persuaded to mount a "reconnaissance-in-force."

The British prime minister's military advisers assured him that, in addition to the international demands for a diversionary action in Europe, the launching of a major assault was of strategic necessity—even if it fell short of a full invasion. In fact, they said, it would not be possible to mount the ultimate invasion without first testing Hitler's Channel defences in France, and testing Allied invasion techniques and equipment.

And so a plan was conceived. With pressure from Canadian military leaders and politicians, it soon also solved Mackenzie King's problem of what to do with the restless Second Division.

Lord Louis Mountbatten

A plan was drawn up by Combined Operations, under Lord Louis Mountbatten . . .

"I proposed to use commandos and the Royal Marine Division, all of whom were battle-trained and experienced men. To my surprise and consternation I was then told that a political decision had been made on the highest level to use Canadian troops, who had been kicking their heels about in England and wanted to get into action. The Second Canadian Division was chosen—an admirable division of excellent, well-trained men. Not any of them had any battle experience. I complained and said this is rather like teaching people to swim by throwing them in at the deep end of the pool."

. . .and a target was selected . . .

Dieppe

Dieppe, showing the beach and the Casino just before the Germans demolished the far wing of the Casino prior to the raid

"You've got to start one day fighting the enemy but you don't start by landing frontally in daylight at a defended port like Dieppe."
—Lord Lovat,
No. 4 Commando

Dieppe was 110 kilometres across the Channel—just within range of British fighter planes, which could form a protective air umbrella over the landing of 6,000 troops and fifty tanks. The objective was to capture this German-occupied port on the Normandy coast and hold it for twelve hours, and then to withdraw with German prisoners, with information about German defences and with the proof of whether or not a combined-forces operation could be made to work under modern conditions. Before Dieppe, one of the last such amphibious assaults attempted had been the disaster at Gallipoli in World War I.

"The Chiefs of Staff rejected my idea of two encircling movements landing each side of Dieppe and coming in behind the city. Instead they wished to have a frontal assault on Dieppe itself. I agreed, providing they had a sufficiently strong aerial bombardment to support this."

Lord Louis Mountbatten,
Chief, Combined Operations

Maj. Gen. John Hamilton Roberts, commander of the Second Canadian Division

"I talked to Leigh-Mallory, my air adviser, and he said the chances of even hitting Dieppe are small, let alone of hitting the targets you want. And so I said no, we wouldn't take the chance because if they could only hit Dieppe, and not the headlands and places where I wanted them to bomb, all it would do would be to block the streets and my tanks would never get through."

Maj.-Gen. John H. Roberts,
Commander, Second Division

German wire on the top of the sea wall at Dieppe

There were too many cooks . . .

"I think the plan was too minute, right down to the last detail. And when so many things cannot be foreseen, you then can't adjust. You've got no alternatives. And I think a plan like that, planned too long ahead of time, is bound to fail. And that's what happened."

Brigadier Gen. Dollard Menard,
Fusiliers Mont-Royal

Maj. Ernest Magnus, Canadian Planning Staff

"The detailed plan was done by our own planning staff—the Canadian Planning Staff at Force Headquarters."

Major Ernest Magnus,
Canadian Planning Staff

Reconnaissance photograph of Dieppe taken shortly before the raid

. . .and not enough information.

"I would say that the information Combined Ops had was scanty. It was based on aerial photographs and on pictures that had been taken by someone having a holiday at Dieppe before the war. There was very little basic defence information. There were a lot of assumptions."

Major Ernest Magnus,
Canadian Planning Staff

Exercise Yukon, on June 11, was the first dress rehearsal. . .and was a disaster. Lord Louis Mountbatten ordered a second exercise; it did not really prepare the men . . .

Assault landing craft in Exercise Yukon, June 12, 1942

R-boats in Exercise Yukon, June 12, 1942

. . .for what happened on August 19, 1942.

The sandy beaches of southern England were totally different from . . .

New tank landing-craft and the recently produced Churchill tank were to be given their first battle trial at Dieppe. During the practice of Exercise Yukon, the tanks performed excellently on England's sandy shores. Tank commanders naturally expected the same thing to happen at Dieppe, but somehow the reconnaissance photos and the snapshots of pre-war vacationers had failed to show what Normandy beaches were actually like.

Churchill tank on Exercise Yukon, June, 1942

Exercise Yukon, June 12, 1942

. . .the rocky shingle at Dieppe.

On the raid, many tanks never made it off the beach. The large stones that comprised the footing were too much even for the Churchill tanks. Most of the vehicles threw a track or simply got bogged down only a few yards from where they landed.

An R.A.F. film crew recorded the organised disorder of rehearsal.

Exercise Yukon, June 12, 1942

Two months later, German photographs etched the chaos of battle, as lives and equipment were wasted on the Dieppe beach.

War-games are one thing . . .

Exercise Yukon, June 12, 1942

. . .war is another.

Dieppe wounded, August 19, 1942

Each step in the planning brought disaster that much closer . . .

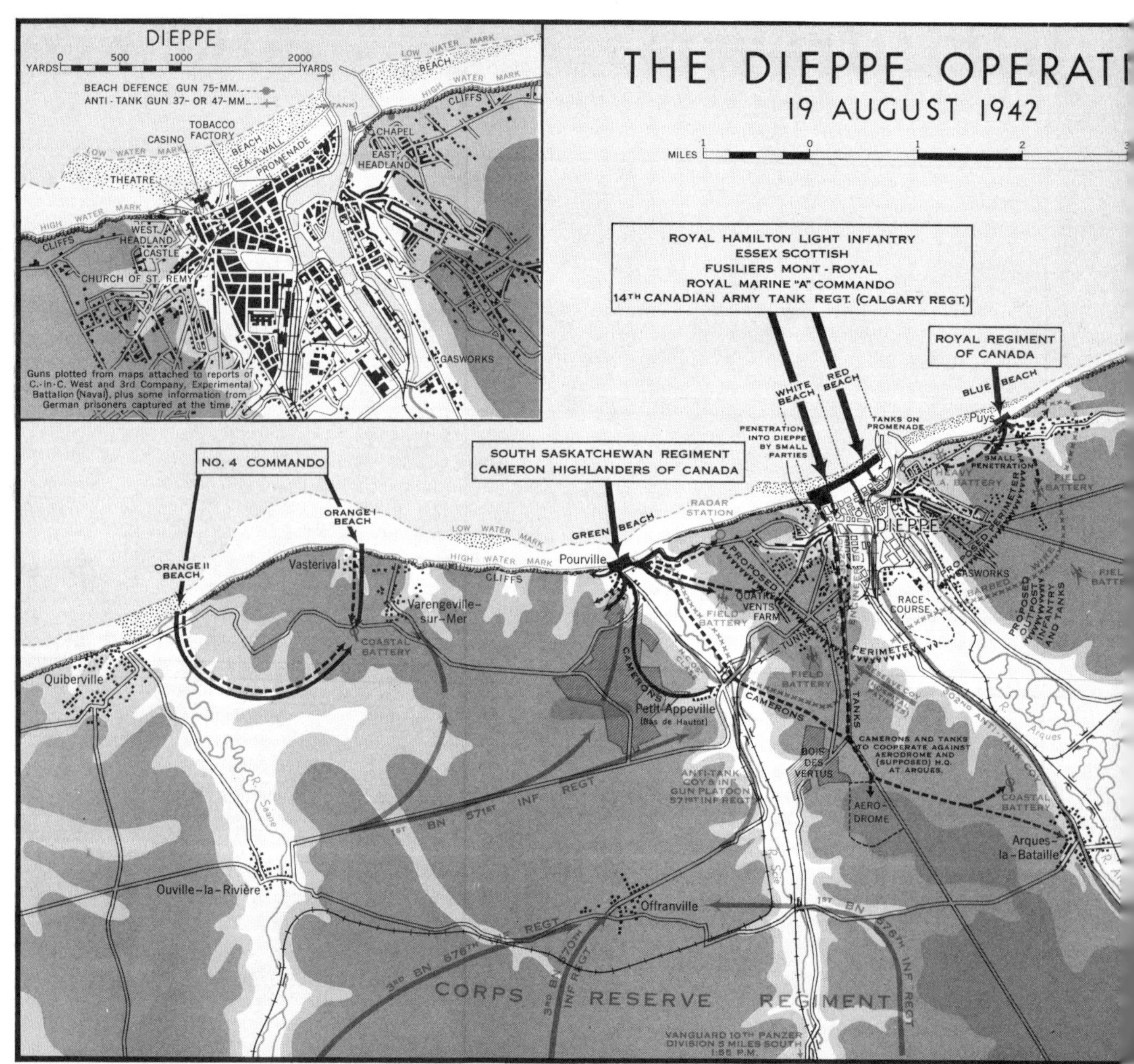

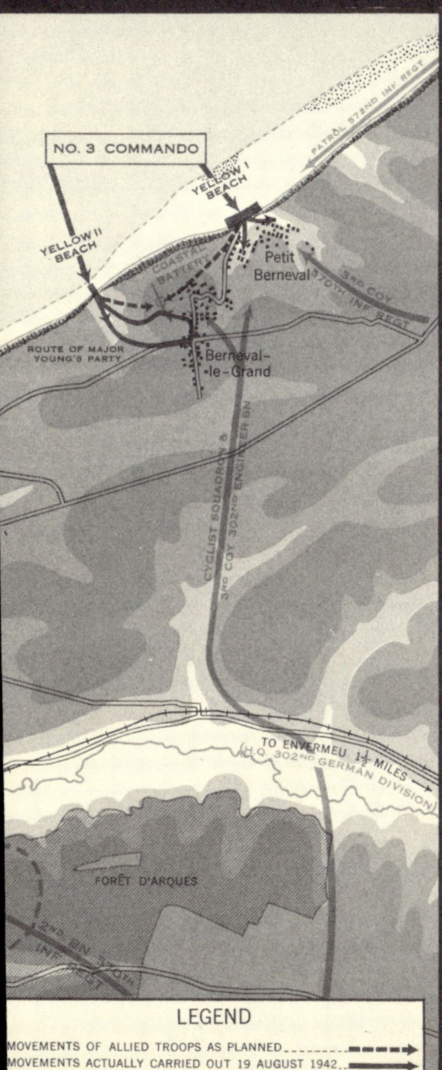

All that was known about German fortifications at Dieppe and its neighbouring resort towns was finally put onto a detailed operations map. There were too many gaps in the information—not just the misconception of the beach's surface, but underestimation of the gun emplacements in caves that riddled the cliffs at either end. The guns were withdrawn into the caves by day, and failed to show up on reconnaissance photographs. They would take a heavy toll on the day of battle.

. . .until the strategy was completed.

This was the order of battle ...and these were the fishing villages and fashionable resorts that would become the battleground....

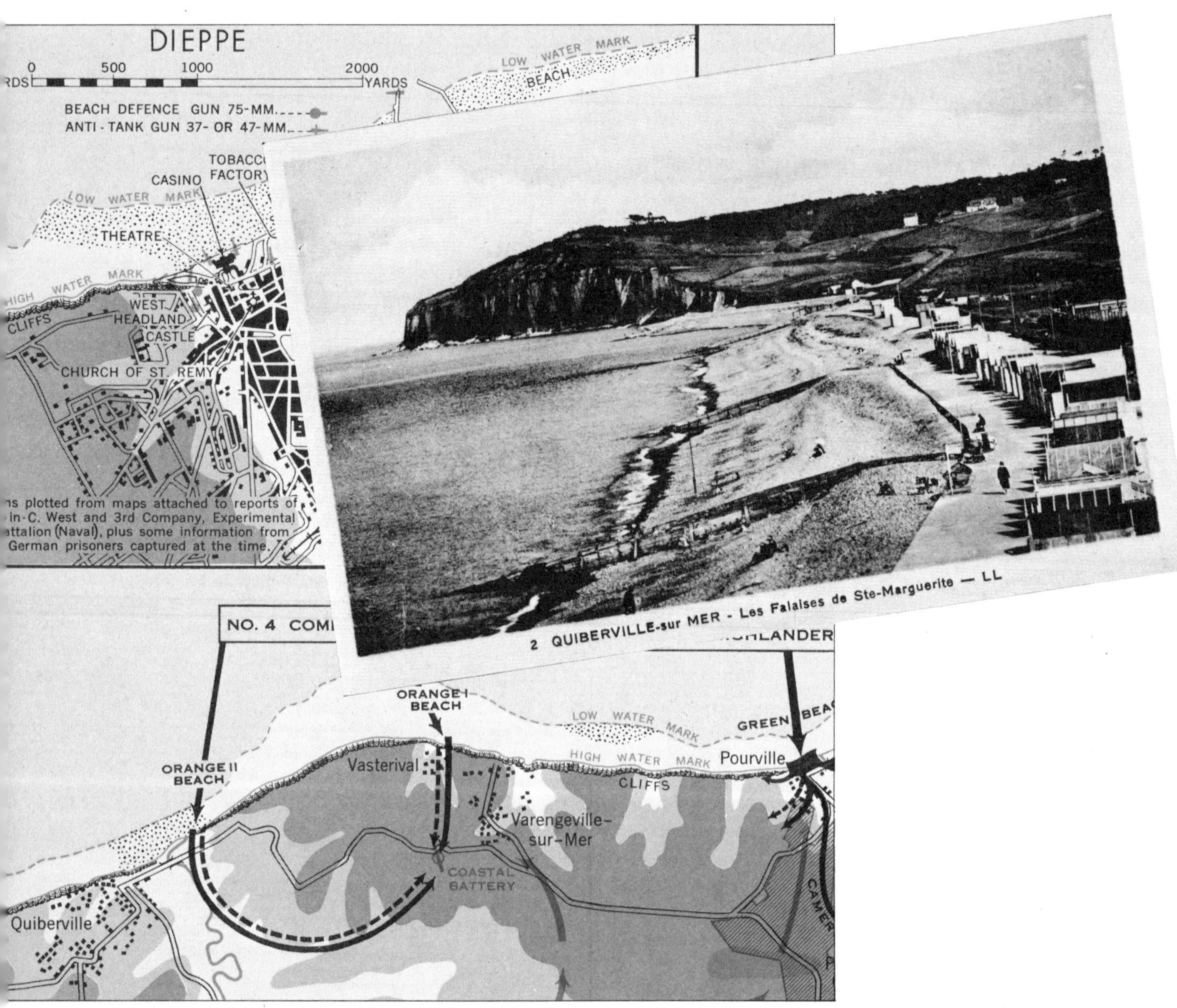

First, the coastal batteries were to be knocked out.

The battleground was made up of a cluster of communities around Dieppe; they were given code names on the battle plan.

Quiberville lay near Orange Beach, the landing site of No. 4 Commando as they were to head inland to destroy one of the large coastal batteries whose big guns posed a threat to the flotilla of landing-craft bringing in the rest of the assault troops and tanks.

Berneval lay to the east of Dieppe. Its coastal battery was to be attacked in another pincer movement—by No. 3 Commando landing at Yellow Beach. Both these British commando units were to attack in darkness—at 04:50, half an hour before the daylight assault on the main beach at Dieppe.

42 BERNEVAL. — L'escalier de Berneval sur mer. — LL.

At the same time, the flanking towns would be attacked.

The small resort of Pourville lay just to the west of Dieppe. It was designated Green Beach. The South Saskatchewan Regiment was to land here at 04:50, occupy the town and sweep on to attack Dieppe's west headland and to raid the radar station that was situated on the way. Half an hour later, the Winnipeg Cameron Highlanders were to land here and move towards an inland rendezvous with the Calgary Tanks, in a joint attack on the aerodrome and on what was mistakenly thought to be German headquarters at Arques-la-Bataille.

Blue Beach lay on the other side of Dieppe at the tiny resort of Puys, destined to be attacked by Toronto's Royal Regiment of Canada. German bunkers on the cliffs, especially those just below the white house on the horizon, would decimate the Royals and prevent them from reaching their objectives—including the guns trained on the beach at Dieppe from the east headland.

OPER
ST 1942
Vue générale
LL 2 POURVILLE
ROYAL REGIMENT OF CANADA
BLUE BEACH
WHITE BEACH
TANKS ON PROMENADE
PENETRATION INTO DIEPPE BY SMALL PARTIES
Puys
SMALL PENETRATION
SOUTH SASKATCHEWAN REGIMENT
CAMERON HIGHLANDERS OF CANADA
ORANGE I BEACH
RADAR STATION
LOW WATER MARK
GREEN BEACH
HIGH WATER MARK
Pourville
CLIFFS
DIEPPE
Varengeville-sur-Mer
COASTAL BATTERY
FIELD BATTERY
QUATRE VENTS FARM
RACE COURSE
GASWORKS
PERIMETER
PROPOSED
1ST BN
3RD BN 676TH
18 PUYS
La Plage

The central target was Dieppe itself . . .

This two-kilometre open stretch was tactically divided into White Beach to the west, where the Royal Hamilton Light Infantry was meant to attack a German stronghold in the Casino before entering the town; and Red Beach to the east, the landing-place of Windsor's Essex Scottish. The Calgary Tanks were to deploy their vehicles all along the beach, and then head through the town to join up with the Cameron Highlanders. Two battalions were to be held offshore in reserve—either to back up the taking of the town or to cover the withdrawal of the troops. These were Britain's Royal Marines and Quebec's Fusiliers Mont-Royal.

. . .but the popular resort had been turned into a German fortress.

WHITE BEACH
RED BEACH
BLU
TANKS ON PROMENADE
NETRATION
NTO DIEPPE
BY SMALL
PARTIES
HEAVY
A.A. BATT
DIEPPE
OSED
ATRE
ENTS
FARM
TUNNE
VUE SUR LE CASINO (R. JOURDE, ARCH.) ET LA PLAGE.
335 DIEPPE

German soldiers preparing trenches and bunkers on the promenade at Dieppe, 1942

For months the Germans had been expecting some sort of Allied action along the Normandy coast. Consequently, they built elaborate fortifications at almost every community along the Channel shore within striking distance from England. A series of concrete bunkers connected by trenches had been constructed on the beach at Dieppe, as a supplement to the machine-gun nests on the cliffs and the anti-tank guns in the cliffs' caves. Barbed wire was strung all along the top of the sea-wall that protected the broad promenade from the Channel surf, and heavy concrete tank barriers blocked every street that led from the frontal boulevard into the town.

German defense exercise, Dieppe, 1942

Alarm drills were held regularly, to keep the German soldiers on their toes.

August 18, 1942 . . .

"We were always on the alert, but the 18th was such a beautiful day my commanding officer said to me, 'We should go down for a swim.' "

German guard at Dieppe, 1942

German soldiers swim at Dieppe, 1942

August 18, 1942: one more training exercise?

Naval forces assembled in ports on England's south shore—Southampton, Portsmouth, Shoreham and here, at Newhaven . . .awaiting British commandos and marines, Canadian infantry and tanks, a few dozen U.S. Rangers—the first Americans to see action in Europe in World War II—and a handful of Free French fighters.

Soon the crowded army vehicles began to roll into the seaside towns.

"We all thought it was just an ordinary exercise. We carried on in the normal way—some without weapons, and so on—because everyone said, 'Well, another exercise again.'"

The original target date for Operation Rutter, as the raid was first called, had been July 8, 1942—but it was called off due to bad weather. The whole mighty assemblage of men and machines had been disbanded. As far as the troops knew, any hope of a Dieppe raid was gone. When military leaders refused to give up the raid, and revived the plan in secret, only some of the senior officers were told. It was too much of a security risk to have 6,000 men hanging around England for a month, waiting for the next set of appropriate tides, knowing that one of the war's biggest raids was about to be launched. . .now code-named Operation Jubilee.

"We landed at Newhaven and discovered from my commanding officer that this was it—we were going into Dieppe. It so happened that I had with me at least five or six people who had not been trained in the original training for the Dieppe raid."

It was the eve of battle.

Landing craft assembling at Newhaven. The young naval officer in the centre, William Sinclair, is now a Justice of the Alberta Supreme Court

The Dieppe flotilla

The air force was standing by to give protective cover.

Seventy squadrons would take to the air in the Dieppe raid, piloted by men from Britain, Canada, Poland, the United States, France, Norway, New Zealand and Czechoslovakia. It would be the mightiest single day of fighter battle in World War II.

Bombers would be flying, as well—not enough to give the kind of softening-up that a daylight frontal attack needed, but enough to keep German planes and anti-aircraft gunners busy.

Loading bombs for the Dieppe raid, August, 1942

Allied pilots with the R.A.F., August, 1942

And then it was 04:50, August 19, 1942. Almost 250 ships silently approached in the pre-dawn darkness.

Zero Hour

No. 4 British Commandos charging through barbed wire at Quiberville. Men threw themselves onto wire, rolled around to press it down, while the rest ran over them

Lord Lovat led No. 4 Commando in the attack on the coastal battery near Orange Beach.

"We had trained ourselves to clear our boats in thirty-five seconds—and that's very fast going for sixty-five men. We were out of the boats, onto the beach and into the wire before the Germans got the range.

"Certain chosen men who were in leather jerkins went forward to the wire which was about six feet high and fully eight feet deep. And the men in leather jerkins literally charged into it like a herd of rogue elephants and rolled about and tried to flatten it...which they did with considerable effect."

One of his men won the Victoria Cross in the raid on Dieppe—Maj. Pat Porteous:

"I started climbing over the wire. When I jumped down the other side—there was quite a bit of a drop—I had a couple of grenades in each pocket. That proved too much for my braces, which gave way. And so I had slight problems in keeping my trousers up for the rest of the operation."

Lord Lovat and his party of men ran inland for almost a mile from their landing point on the beach at Quiberville—in order to be in position to attack the big guns from the rear once a second party of No. 4 Commando reached the battery from Orange I Beach, at Vasterival.

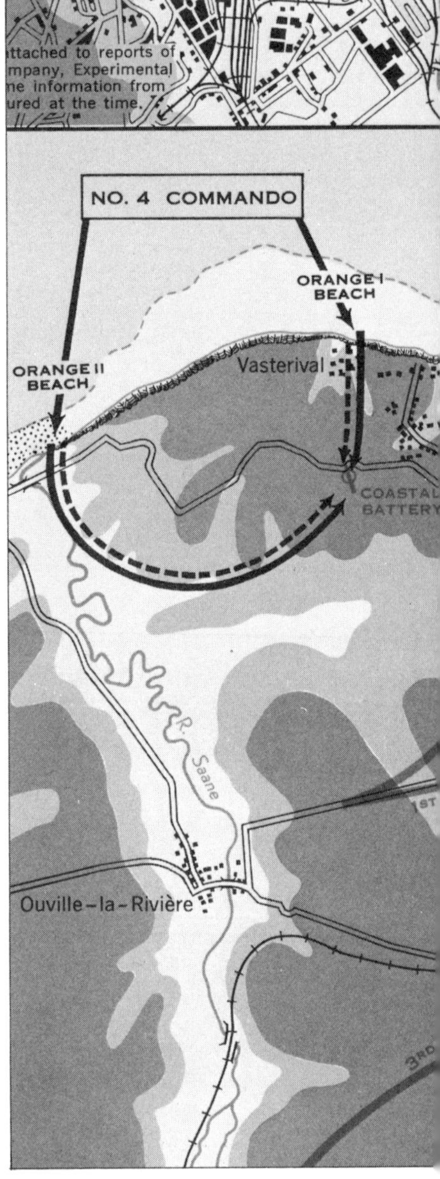

Lord Lovat, leader of No. 4 Commando at Dieppe, went on the raid with his hunting rifle

Pat Porteous and Lord Lovat

Maj. Pat Porteous of No. 4 Commando, winner of the Victoria Cross at Dieppe

Franklin Koons, a U.S. Ranger in the Dieppe raid, beside the ruins of the barn where a No. 4 Commando sniper was hidden; the sniper killed the layer of No. 1 gun

Maj. Derek Mills-Roberts led the second party inland.

"And there in front of us lay the battery, large as life. And then we came along to a barn, and taking one of our snipers we ran up onto the first floor, and settled him on a convenient table. We could see the big guns in front of us, all the gun crews there with not a suspicion—a beautiful summer's day, the odd bee buzzing. . .nothing at all. And I said to my sniper, kill the layer behind the number-one gun. And then he got himself on the table, and got himself into a comfortable position—rather as they do at Bisley—and after an awesome and lengthy process of time. . .the rifle cracked. The layer fell into the gun-pit with tremendous surprise all round."

"One thing that was a bit of a pity—we couldn't get our three-inch mortar firing. But within a comparatively short time, Sgt.-Maj. Dunning came up with his little two-inch mortar. . ."

No. 4 Commando attacking German heavy gun battery at Varengeville

A direct hit on the ammunition dump... and one of the guns was a write-off.

Derek Mills-Roberts today

"The Verey light meant that Lovat's men were charging from the other side. . ."

"One troop of sixty men came in from one side, the other came from straight behind. They attacked with fixed bayonets. The fight was short, furious, with no quarter asked or given. It was all over within three to five minutes."

"And then in came the *Messerschmidts,* flying very low. And of course this was an embarrassment as far as we were concerned. So, instead of bolting we got up and waved. And Lord Lovat—a tall figure—gave a very genial wave and I remember the squadron leader waggled his wings and waved. . .and that was that. It passed off quite nicely. It could have been awkward."

No. 4 Commando withdrawing from Orange Beach

"It was a long carry back to the boats."

"They seemed one hell of a long way off, and before we were entirely clear, we were being shot at from the tops of these cliffs."

"We laid smoke-screens which had been practised in training, and we got the wounded onto the boats and away in pretty quick time."

No. 4 Commando on the way back to England heading to pick up a downed American Spitfire pilot

"It's rather like a bank robbery—a commando raid: you get in all right but it's the getting out that's the tricky part."

No. 4 Commando withdrawing from Orange Beach

No. 4 Commando jubilant on the way back to England

No. 4 Commando returned to England. . .triumphant.

No. 4 Commando arrive back in England

Lord Lovat's strategy had paid off.

Rather than entrusting the detailed planning of his action to Combined Operations, Lord Lovat devised his own tactics—based on his considerable experience with commando raids up and down the coast of Europe. This, together with the fact that his men were almost all battle-hardened, provided his No. 4 Commando with a victorious day on August 19, 1942.

Lord Lovat, leader of No. 4 Commando

No. 4 Commando arrive back in England

The U.S. Rangers were impressed.

Fifty Rangers took part in the Dieppe raid—the first American soldiers to fight in Europe in World War II. Some saw action with No. 4 Commando, including Sgt. Alex Szima.

"A sniper took the hat off my head—put a hole through the stocking cap—put a bullet through the troop sergeant-major and killed the aid man that came to help him by putting one through his head. By the time I took cover in a manure pile there were already three additional people on the ground. So this was no fooling around, and at that point I would say I was afraid."

Sgt. Alex Szima, a U.S. Ranger with No. 4 Commando (receiving the light)

Sgt. Franklin Koons—a corporal at Dieppe—was possibly the first American soldier to kill a German in the war and the first to win a decoration: the British Military Medal.

"Our commander, Lord Lovat, came by and slapped me on the shoulder and said, 'How are you doing, Yank? How'd you like the show?' And I was pretty happy and I said, 'I liked it real well, I think we're headed back for good!' "

Sgt. Franklin Koons, a Corporal at Dieppe, was one of the first American soldiers to kill a German in World War II. He is being decorated with the British Military Medal by Lord Louis Mountbatten

Experience paid off for No. 3 Commando when bad luck hit. . . .

Another commando party headed for the coastal battery to the east of Dieppe, near Yellow Beach at Berneval. At about 03:00 their arm of the Allied armada ran into a small German convoy, also heading for Dieppe. In the ensuing skirmish many of the landing-craft went off course in the darkness. Only a few boatloads of No. 3 Commando managed to touch down on the two beaches that were to be the origins of another pincer attack, and of these landing parties, only one boatload—led by Maj. Peter Young—was successful in scaling the cliffs and reaching the big guns.

Their rugged training had prepared them for the cliffs at Yellow Beach.

British Commandos training

No. 3 Commando climbing cliff at Berneval (the top man on cliff is Maj. Peter Young)

Maj. Peter Young at cliffs

Maj. Peter Young and his men saved the day at Berneval. . . .

"The first thing we did was to go up to the cliff and have a pee, actually—there was no accommodation in the landing-craft. We then trooped along to the gap in the cliff, expecting to be fired at from up the gully. Nothing happened. . .and I started climbing up the cliff. The Germans had pegged in their wire the whole way up—the only foothold was their pegs. . .

"I thought, 'Oh Christ, if I fall off this time I shan't have the guts to start climbing again.' I just hung on by my eyebrows and up we went. It took about twenty minutes."

During the attack, German reinforcements arrived on bicycles.

Peter Young and his two dozen men could not hope to destroy the gun battery at Berneval, but by judicious sniping they managed to draw the big guns' fire away from the ships offshore. . .during the rest of the landings.

And then they headed home.

German cyclist troops heading for Berneval

"Actually, we had a hilarious voyage back to Newhaven!"

"We were picked up by Mr. Fear and his M.L., and he took us on board and greeted us warmly and gave us rum. . .or whiskey. . .or both!"

"I remember Peter Young putting his arm around my neck and saying, 'You're the Queen of the Navy,' and I thought, 'My Christ, we've got seventy miles to go yet!' "

No. 3 Commando on the way back to England (Maj. Peter Young in the centre)

Alex Fear's motor launch attacked the Franz, an armed German tanker . . .

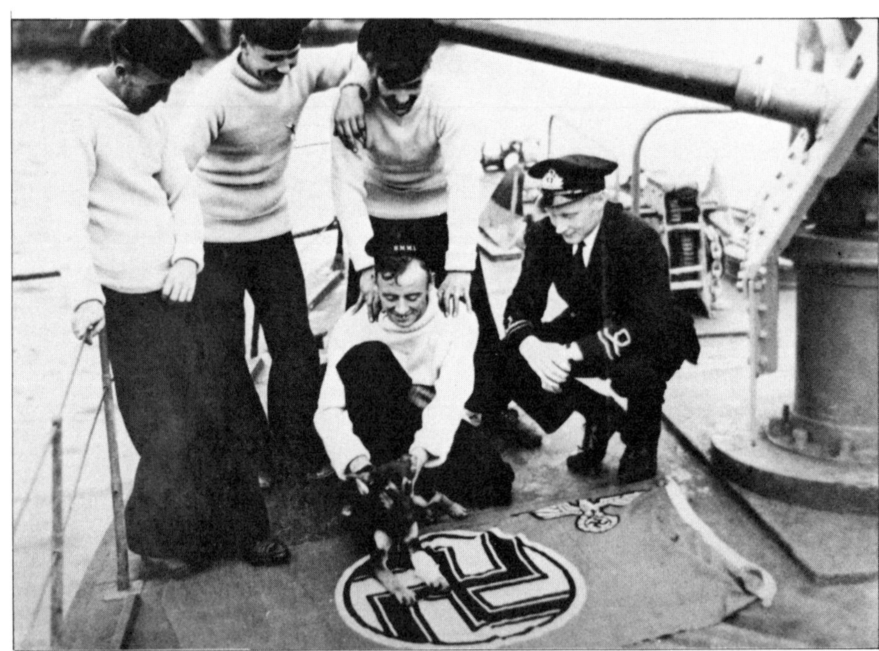

Lt. Alex Fear (on the right) with the flag of the German boat which he and his crew attacked during the raid

. . .and then took the commandos home.

No. 3 Commando back in England (a censor has scratched the photograph to remove the "3" from the shoulder badge on the right)

No. 3 Commando back in England

“I remember thinking, ‘My God, what’s going to happen next?’ ”

“There was all the brass in Newhaven, waiting, because we were the first boat back. And Peter Young and I walked up the quay arm in arm—he was in his bare feet—and we just brushed them all aside, walked into the mess and sat down and had a couple of pints. And with all the top brass waiting there for the news, we just ignored them.”

Alex Fear today

No. 3 Commando back in England

"And that was really the way we came back!"

Richard Schnösenberg today

Reg Hall on the beach at Puys, 1978

Bad luck at Puys was disastrous for the Royals.

While the British commandos had been making their pre-dawn landings near the two coastal batteries, Canadian infantry battalions had been meant to touch down at two small resorts flanking Dieppe itself. Toronto's Royal Regiment of Canada was supposed to reach the beach at Puys at 04:50, but they, too, were delayed by the encounter with the German convoy. Day was just breaking when they made what was supposed to be a surprise attack—but the German defences were fully manned, by order of Richard Schnösenberg:

"On the night of the 18th, I had called a practice alert for my battalion, not knowing that this alert would actually involve the British and the Canadians."

Reg Hall was one of the Royals who landed in an inescapable cross-fire.

"We all dashed off the landing-craft into a hail of bullets. The three men in front of me went down within a few yards, and we just dashed for the cliffs."

Machine-gun nests on the cliffs above and at the white house in the background completely covered the beach, while hand grenades thrown down from the cliffs blasted the huddled survivors.

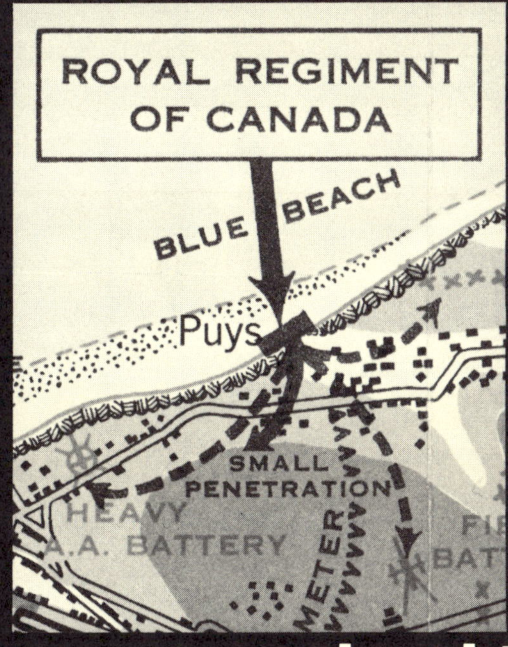

Puys was a slaughter.

Royal Regiment of Canada being slaughtered by cross fire at Puys

Canadian dead at Puys, August 19, 1942

Almost 500 young Canadians had been plunged into a death-trap.

The Reverend Michael Boultbee was a young naval rating who could see the slaughter from his landing-craft:

"I wouldn't know how many survived more than a matter of minutes, because by this time everything was happening. The noise of gun-fire was all around. I can't imagine they would have got more than a few yards up the beach."

Reverend Michael Boultbee today

German defenses at Puys, August, 1942

Part of the Royal Regiment of Canada surrendering at Puys, August 19, 1942

"All of a sudden a German officer appeared. . . ."

"He said, 'It's all right, boys, your commander has surrendered. Put down your arms and all your ammunition, and march out.' And then we all got up and marched out. And the battle was over."

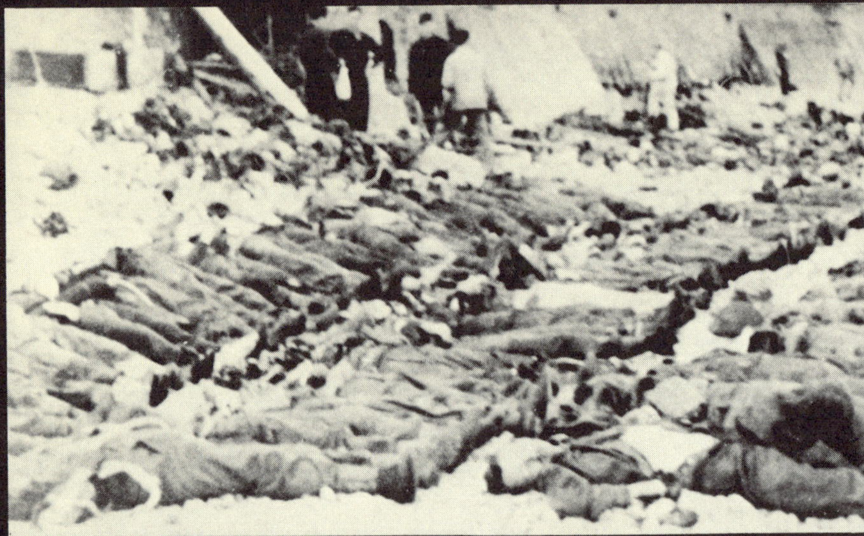

Canadian dead at Puys, August 19, 1942

Two hundred and twenty-five Canadians lay dead.

Canadian prisoners of war at Puys, August 19, 1942

Two hundred and sixty-four were taken prisoner.

West headland at Puys, at the end of the war

Bitter memories haunt the beach at Puys.

"So many good chaps were killed. You spent your life with them—right from Toronto and right through all the training in England. And all of a sudden you didn't have anybody left at all. You felt so alone."

The Royal Regiment of Canada had been almost wiped out of existence.

Of those who landed here, only three made it back to England that day.

East headland at Puys at the end of the war

German bunker at top of the stairs on the east headland at Puys

SOUTH SASKATCHEWAN REGIMENT
CAMERON HIGHLANDERS OF CANADA
RADAR STATION
GREEN BEACH
LOW WATER MARK
HIGH WATER MARK
Pourville
CLIFFS
FIELD BATTERY
CAMERONS
N.C.O.S' CLASS
Petit Appeville
(Bas de Hautot)
ANTI-TANK COY & INF GUN PLATOON 571ST INF REGT
INF REGT

Col. Cecil Merritt led the S.S.R's across the bridge at Pourville.

*Col. Cecil Merritt of the South
Saskatchewan Regiment
winning VC for standing on
bridge under fire at Pourville
and encouraging his men to
cross*

The South Saskatchewans were on time at Pourville . . .

At 04:50, just before dawn, the S.S.R's touched down at Pourville, just to the west of Dieppe. The Germans here were caught off guard, and the first waves of Canadians quickly penetrated the town. One party was to capture the west headland while others moved to their objectives up the valley of the River Scie and on towards Dieppe, in the direction of a radar station to the east.

However, in order to reach the east headland of Pourville, the S.S.R's first had to cross the river, and it was at the bridge over the Scie that the enemy fire became deadly.

. . .until they reached the bridge at the east end of town.

By this time, German gunners on the cliffs ahead had the bridge completely covered by machine-guns and mortars. Some of the Canadians managed to get over, while others fell under the relentless fire from the heights. A few managed to clamber across on the girders underneath:

"That's how we got across the river, but nobody said to move on anywhere else, so we decided we'd better go back. So back we went through the girders onto the other side."

Those on the far side were in danger of being cut off; the attack had lost its impetus. There was stalemate and confusion when the colonel of the S.S.R, Cecil Merritt, reached the bridge and tried to talk his men into making another rush across it. Some of those who had scattered to take cover were separated from their officers, and therefore had no idea what their objectives were on the other side.

"There was no sense to go across the bridge, other than the colonel was calling for us to go, and as privates, we should have gone. But we just didn't have the enthusiasm to go, and we had been over the fool bridge twice already—or under it—and back again. And there was nothing on the other side to do. So that was where we stopped."

Pourville bridge today

Colonel Merritt braved the bullets to get his men over the bridge . . .

"When Colonel Merritt saw us stop, he said, 'What's the matter with you fellows? You're not frightened, are you?' And without waiting for an answer he said, 'Come out here.' So I walked out in the middle of the road, with great trepidation, and he swung his helmet on the forefinger of his left hand and said, 'You see? There's no fire out here!' "

The men of the S.S.R. finally made their move—but it was too late. Their attack to the east had fallen short of its objectives, as had their push into the head of the Scie Valley.

. . .and became one of the two Canadians to win the Victoria Cross at Dieppe.

"I think Merritt richly deserved his V.C., but not only for the bridge. Every bloody soldier in our regiment saw him that day . . .and that took some guts!"

Maj. Claude Orme was also one of the heroes of the day.

He led the attack up onto the west headland of Pourville.

"We eventually arrived at our objective, and so I thought it was about time to send the code word, 'Sorry.' I discovered later on that apart from Lord Lovat's signal, it was the only success signal sent to the headquarters ship during the operation."

Viscount Alexander decorates Maj. Claude Orme of the S.S.R. who led his men in taking their objective on the west headland at Pourville

R-boats off Dieppe, August 19, 1942

A Boston bomber laying smoke off the beach at Pourville

The Cameron Highlanders followed the S.S.R.'s in . . .

The Winnipeg regiment arrived half an hour later, in daylight, to sweep along the path that the S.S.R.'s were to have cleared for them—up the valley to an inland meeting point where they were to join up with the Calgary Tanks.

By the time the Highlanders drew near the shore, the battle had been raging long enough to fill the air with bullets.

"It was like the 24th of May, the stuff that was coming out at us. We were informed the night before that the coast was to be bombed and we were more or less clean-up men. Instead of this, the shoe was on the other foot. They were cleaning us up as we went in. And it was hell, I'll tell you."

. . .to the tune of "One Hundred Pipers."

"I looked to my right and there stood a man on the craft next to me, with a Highland bonnet on, ribbons flying in the breeze, and he was playing the bagpipes. And it was the most momentous moment of my life. I've never been so ready to die as I was then."

Piper Alex Graham piping Winnipeg Cameron Highlanders into Pourville while under fire

"I started playing probably a mile offshore, because at the time the motor on our boat had conked out, and the naval officer asked me to keep playing because it was stirring his men, and good for their morale. I continued playing under heavy fire."

Piper Alex Graham kept up the Camerons' spirits. . .but they, too, were unable to reach their objective.

The Highlanders got farther inland than anyone on the raid, but German defences were too heavy to allow them to accomplish much. So, along with the S.S.R.'s, they fought a rearguard action while awaiting evacuation.

(Left) Alex Graham who piped Camerons into Pourville leading veterans past L'Arc de Triomphe, Paris, 1950's

Canadian soldier watching a Boston bomber from the beach at Pourville (photo possibly taken by a British photographer whose film was captured by the Germans)

Some remained behind . . .

The two prairie regiments suffered somewhat lighter casualties than the groups from eastern Canada, but still left many of their comrades on the beach at Pourville, when heavy German fire prevented many of the landing-craft from reaching the shore during the withdrawal.

Petit Appeville, August 19, 1978, ceremony honouring the Camerons

. . .but all are remembered.

Each year the French hold a ceremony at Petit Appeville, the farthest inland point reached by the Queen's Own Cameron Highlanders, to commemorate the brave men who fought on August 19, 1942.

Allied ships off Dieppe during the raid

By the time Allied forces hit the main beach at Dieppe, the armed headlands on either side were supposed to have been taken . . .

"Jesus, we're really getting into something that we didn't plan on!"

. . .but the flanking attacks had failed.

Gun batteries covering the beach from the west were to have been knocked out by the S.S.R., but they were unable to get that far. And to the east the Royals had been stopped at Puys. Thus, two infantry battalions and the Calgary Tanks headed into a fully defended landing. . . .

The beach at Dieppe seen from offshore during the raid

Dieppe from a landing craft during the raid

The Royal Hamilton Light Infantry were pinned down on White Beach, near the Casino. . . .

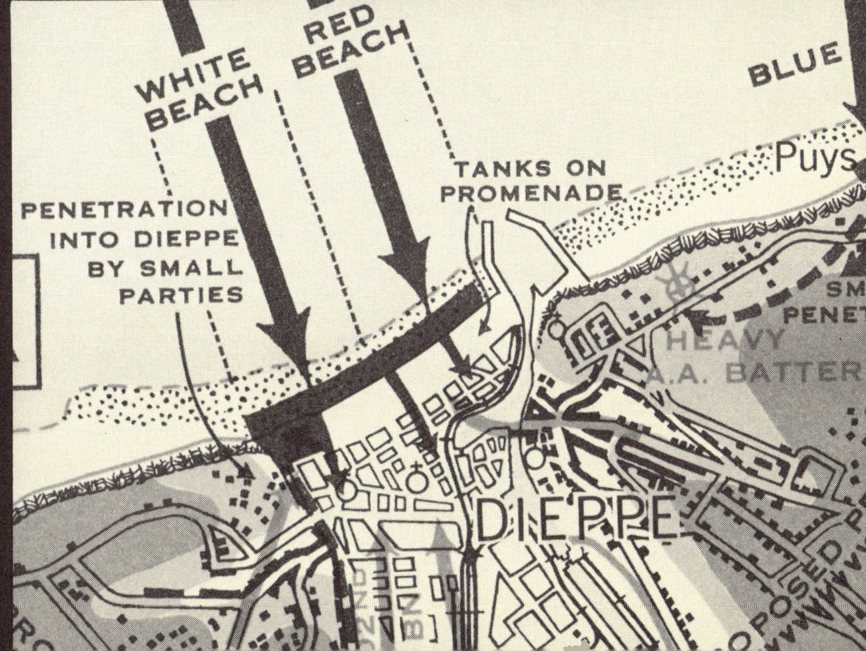

“And then the world hit us!”

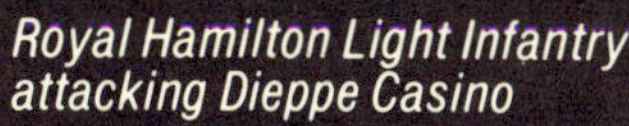

Royal Hamilton Light Infantry attacking Dieppe Casino

"You suddenly realize that you're in hell . . . ."

"Just a smashing, roaring sound—a monstrous sound assails your ears. The earth is shaking."

"Firing from artillery was tremendous, particularly off the east headland where there were caves. These caves were filled with artillery that pounded us to hell."

"I was receiving messages of people being pinned down on the rocks, people being pinned down behind the wall, of terrible mortar fire and machine-gun fire coming down at them. . . ."

Herbert Titzmann was one of the German gunners . . .

"I knew as an infantryman I wouldn't have wanted to be in the place of those Canadians, lying on those damned stones, not only having the fire come at them but with fragments of stone flying everywhere."

Herbert Titzmann today

. . .as some of the R.H.L.I. reached the Casino.

"We just crawled along the sea-wall and when we got inside the Casino it was a shambles. There were dead Germans, there were some of our people wounded and dead, there were Germans that had already been captured and tied up."

Tank landing craft on the way in to Dieppe

Landing craft with Bren gun carrier waiting to go in to Dieppe. Their LCM was never sent in

Meanwhile the Calgary Tanks were heading in to the beach. . . .

Ed Bennett commanded one of the tanks. . . .

"I was standing on the back of my tank just behind the turret when there was a terrific explosion."

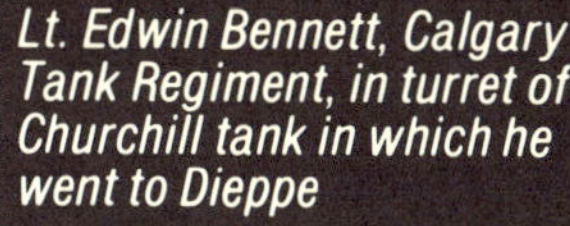

Lt. Edwin Bennett, Calgary Tank Regiment, in turret of Churchill tank in which he went to Dieppe

Archie Anderson was in his crew.

"And this explosion swathed Mr. Bennett in a sheet of flames."

"I reached up, my hair was crisp and my face was burned. Soon I couldn't see very well."

"He was losing a lot of blood, and he said 'Can you take the tank in?' And I swallowed a very large lump and said, 'Yes, sir, I think so.' Then he said, 'Never mind, I can go myself.'"

"I just had time to get back into the tank and off we went."

Archie Anderson then

Archie Anderson today

Edwin Bennett today

"As we left the Tank Landing Craft there was a circle of wounded men on the beach. . . ."

"They were all gathered in a circle as though they were trying to help each other and doing what they could for themselves. And then like a film break a shell landed among them and when the flash disappeared, so had they."

"I think I would have to say at that point I felt sheer terror."

Calgary tanks (Ed Bennett's 'Bellicose') landing at Dieppe

Tanks stranded near the Casino at Dieppe

The tanks were completely wasted on the beach at Dieppe.

Only a few managed to cross the stones of the beach without throwing a track, but even those that got across the anti-tank ditch and over the sea-wall onto the promenade were stopped. Concrete barriers blocked all entrances to the town. There was nothing to do but use the tanks as pill-boxes, and fire at the Germans until it was time to withdraw.

Tank with a thrown track in front of the Casino at Dieppe

Allied ships off Dieppe during the raid

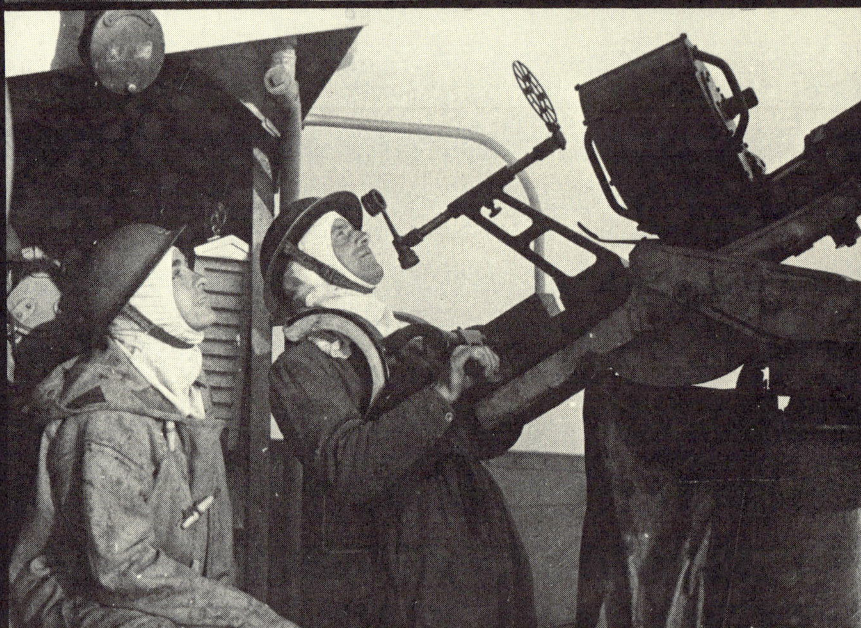

Anti-aircraft gun aboard one of the Allied ships

By now, the offshore flotillas were under attack from the air.

The battle plan had been modified to eliminate heavy bombing of Dieppe, but R.A.F. Spitfires and Hurricanes were engaging *Luftwaffe* planes in a giant dogfight five miles high and twenty-five miles across.

Allied planes over Dieppe during the raid

Luftwaffe plane

It was the biggest fighter battle of any single day in the war.

The Allies lost 106 planes. . .in one of the war's worst days. They claimed 170 German planes destroyed or damaged. The fact was that only 48 *Luftwaffe* planes had been shot down, and another 24 damaged.

Over 2,000 sorties were flown all day, and immediately relived . . .

. . .by Allied pilots . . .
. . .and by the Luftwaffe.

R.A.F. Boston light bomber over Dieppe

Aerial view of Dieppe during the raid

R.A.F. pilots

German pilots in France

Heinz Klems, Luftwaffe pilot

Heinz Klems flew a FW190 against the R.A.F. fighters:

"There were about a hundred Spitfires over Dieppe, and we had to pierce the air umbrella that was protecting the landing. It was a tough assignment."

"In the whole battle, it was quite indecisive as to who had supremacy in the air."

The beach at Dieppe during the raid

German gunners at Dieppe during the raid

There was still a stalemate on the beach at Dieppe.

Windsor's Essex Scottish had landed on Red Beach, in the eastern half of the open stretch. Without any shelter but the sea-wall, few of them managed to get more than several yards beyond it. German firing was unceasing.

Miraculously, a dozen Essex Scottish penetrated the town, led by Company Sergeant-Major Cornelius Stapleton.

Dave Hart, R.C.S., 1978

"Well, we decided—just one mad dash—straight across the promenade. One mad dash."

Con Stapleton and his men spent five hours in Dieppe, killed a few of the enemy and returned to the beach. But before they came back their exploit had been reported in a message first picked up by David Hart.

"I did get a message back from the Essex Scottish saying that one of their people had penetrated the town. I passed this back to Force Headquarters, and I think somewhere along the line this was translated into the fact that the whole Essex Scottish were in the town."

Cornelius Stapleton on beach he crossed in penetrating the town

Cornelius Stapleton in a street in Dieppe where he and a dozen of his fellow Essex Scottish eluded German capture

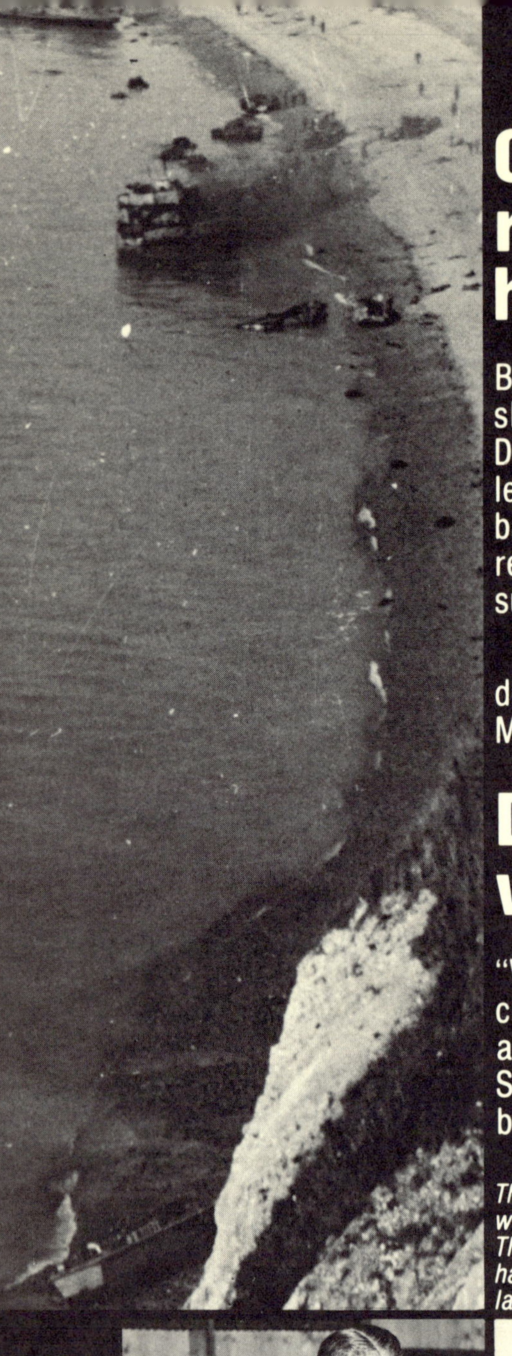

One word dropped from a radio message. . .and hundreds more would die.

By the time the message had been passed to the headquarters ship, H.M.S. *Calpe,* it no longer read "Twelve Essex Scottish in Dieppe." The first word became garbled in transmission, leading General Roberts to believe that he had a whole battalion in the town. He immediately ordered in the floating reserves to back up what he understood to be the first sign of success on the main beach.

Consequently, more brave men were thrown into the death-trap at Dieppe—the Royal Marines and Les Fusiliers Mont-Royal, led by Dollard Menard.

Dollard Menard's F.M.R. were doomed from the start.

"We got into the smoke-screen and the people in charge of the craft didn't know where we were. So some of the troops landed away to the right, under the cliffs—they became useless. Some were out on the left—the wrong place—and they became useless. And the remainder landed in the middle."

The west end of the beach where some F.M.R.'s landed. The Germans threw down hand grenades on these landing craft

 Gen. Roberts, Commander, Dieppe

Landing craft bringing in reinforcements to Dieppe

H.M.S. Calpe, *the headquarters ship, off Dieppe during the raid, laying down a smoke screen*

Les Fusiliers Mont Royal landing at Red Beach

Dollard Menard, who led les Fusiliers Mont Royal at Dieppe

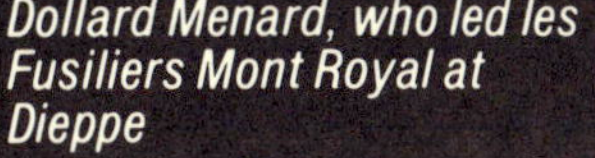

The tide was out—and during the run in and long wade to shore, the F.M.R. massacre began.

'We had to stop along the edge of the water and act dead. I must have spent a good hour in the sea, acting dead. You know—you try to cover your head the best you can from the mortar bombs. And as you land you know there are about a thousand men who've been killed and wounded already. And the edge of the sea is red. No doubt about it—it is Canadian blood. It is a very bad sight to see. It's a thing you keep in your mind all the rest of your life."

Canadian dead on the beach at Dieppe

"I jumped into water maybe knee-high, with a signals operator. I spoke to him—no answer. I turned around—he'd been shot."

"So I walked onto the beach and I saw these soldiers lying on the ground, with their heads pointed towards the wall as if they were getting ready for something. So I waited for them to do something—but they didn't move. So I crawled over to one of them, turned him over, spoke to him—he was dead. I checked a few more. They were all dead."

"We had no cover. We couldn't dig in the pebbles—it was just like trying to make a hole in water. You just can't do it. We had no protection. We were in a cross-fire from the two high sides of the beach and a frontal fire which covered the whole beach. We were just pinned down. We couldn't walk back, we couldn't get forward, we couldn't go on the sides. We were dead, really, before dying."

Dollard Menard's experience was repeated all over the beach. A few of his men made it to the Casino, and from there, along with some of the R.H.L.I., into the town. There was little that such small parties could do there, so they withdrew to the beach. The hours passed—until finally the signal came that the landing-craft were about to make an attempt to reach the beach for the evacuation.

The withdrawal was chaos.

"There was a mad rush for the boats. There were far too many men for the boats, which just went under with the weight of the bodies. They literally threw themselves into the water. They came over the doors, they came over the side of the boat. And as the boat was rocking, these dead bodies were coming in. They were shot coming through the doors."

"I remember seeing bodies at the water's edge, rolling back and forth with the surf. You could tell where the craft had come in because there were groups of bodies at a given point—where a craft had loaded."

"And yes, you could actually smell the sweet smell of the blood."

"The assistant beach master came up from the edge of the water and said, 'That's the last boat.' I said, 'What do you mean, that's the last boat?' He said, 'I mean just what I say, that's the last boat.' I said, 'What are we going to do?' And I remember, he just shrugged his shoulders and looked at me."

Landing craft sinking with door stuck down

ALC
6

H.M.S. Berkeley *sinking off Dieppe with a Spitfire plunging into the sea*

Lofty Haynes today

H.M.S. Berkeley received a direct hit . . .

One of the destroyer's pom-pom gunners was Lofty Haynes:

"This German plane had come over the cliff top, chased by two Spitfires. It was a point-blank shot. I knocked the wings right off, and I remember now all those silver bombs coming down—he had opened the bomb doors, he couldn't have aimed for us—and about four hit us."

"It lifted the ship right out of the water, and all the poor chaps down below—the wounded we'd picked up—went down with it. I don't think there could have been many survivors. There couldn't have been."

H.M.S. Berkeley *sinking off Dieppe*

. . .and had to be sunk once the survivors were rescued.

Evacuation of crew of H.M.S. Berkeley

H.M.S. Berkeley *sunk by a Royal Navy torpedo to prevent her drifting ashore*

The armada straggled home . . .

Six hundred of those who made it back were wounded

The lucky ones who made it to a boat

Picking up survivors

. . .picking up downed air-men and soldiers who had swum out from the beaches.

Survivors transfer from a landing craft to one of the mother ships

The flotilla limps home

YZ
CD 04

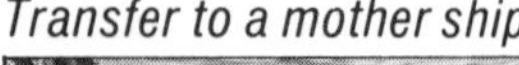
Transfer to a mother ship

Only a thousand were rescued from the beaches . . .

. . .600 of them wounded.

"I'd never seen so many or such serious casualties before. There was a great deal of blood. And the gangways of the ship towards the end of the operation were literally filled with bodies in various stages of injury and disablement."

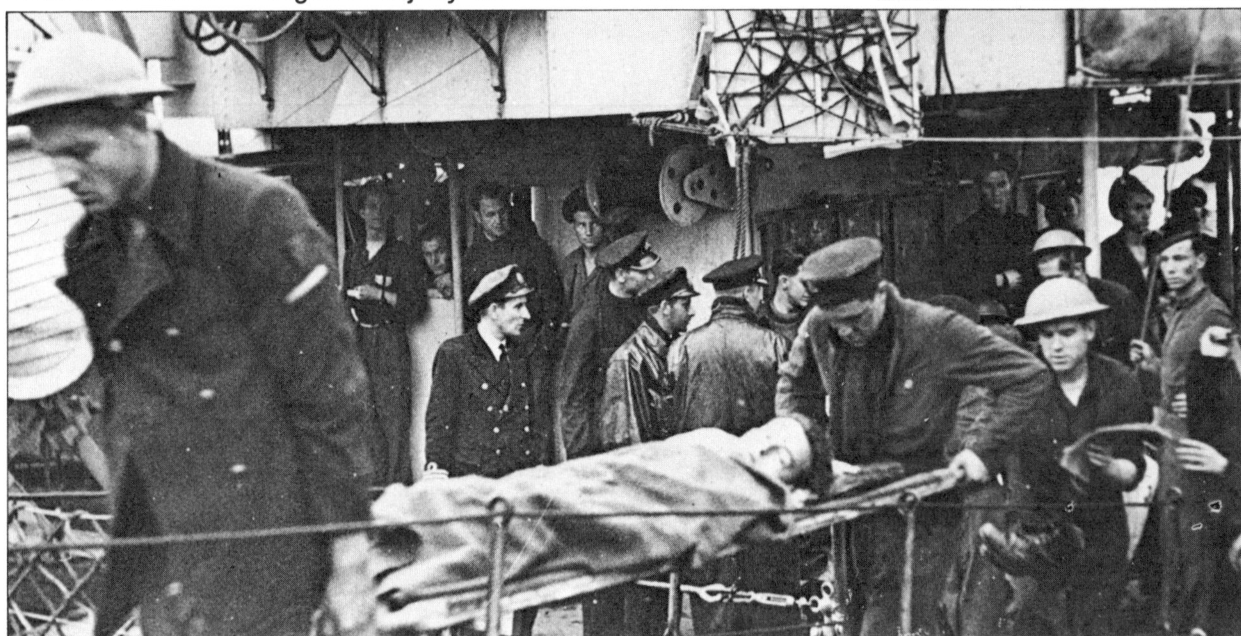

The wounded leave a Polish destroyer—the Slazak

Third from the left is one of the Free French who fought at Dieppe

Very few German prisoners were brought back.

A German P.O.W. brought back from Dieppe

Surviving Canadians went off to hospital, or to half-empty camps.

A blindfolded German prisoner of war arrives at Newhaven

On the way to a British hospital

THE WEATHER
Cloudy and Warm

The Hamilton Spectator

HOME EDITION

VOL. XCVI—NO. 193 | 24 PAGES | HAMILTON CANADA WEDNESDAY AUGUST 19 1942 | PRICE TWO CENTS

CANADIAN TROOPS LEAD GREAT COMMANDO RAID

Gains Made Since May 15 Cost Huns 1,250,000 Men; Stalingrad Assault Looms

Germans Bolster Forces for Full-Scale Drive—

Land With Tanks, Heavy Weapons; Wage Fierce Fight With Boches In Dynamic Dieppe Area Attack

Even before the fighting had finished, the propaganda had begun.

Radio listeners at home heard the excited voices of war correspondents who had been on the scene. . . .

"In the middle of the morning I stepped ashore for a few minutes on this beach. . .but I found myself almost alone. The main body of Canadians was fighting in the town by that time, and the beach was just a bleak place which had been fought over."

"Dieppe was always a great spot for honeymoon couples, but on the day of this great raid it was a grand spot for Canadian troops and their tanks. For hours, Dieppe was theirs. They held the town, created a great deal of damage there, captured numerous German prisoners and then retreated in perfect order."

British reports understandably concentrated on the success of the British commandos, while the American press, ignoring both the Canadians and the fact that only fifty U.S. Rangers took part in the raid, proclaimed, "We and the British invade France!"

LEARN AT DIEPPE ALLIES CAN LAND WHEN THEY WILL

Force Germans on 24-Hour Alert From Narvik to Brest

BIGGER RAIDS YET

London, Aug. 20—Canadians and their Allied comrades have returned from Dieppe with a clear and complete picture of the enemy defences on the most strongly fortified stretch of the French coast and the knowledge that, under an umbrella of planes, they can land in Europe at will.

It may be assumed that as the result of this dress rehearsal for a full scale invasion, the entire formidable Germany army in western Europe will be forced on a 24-hour-a-day alert from now on, from the Brest peninsula to Narvik on the Norwegian coast, 1,800 miles to the north.

The toughest troops of four nations proved that the second front is feasible.

Can Open Second Front

Military quarters, assessing the results of the raid they regard as a complete and inspiring success, said:

1—It proved that a second front can be opened in the west at a price which may be calculated in advance.

2—To open it while half-ready would be suicidal.

3—The raid was effected with the greatest concentration of men weapons and airplanes ever directed against an objective of such size.

4—There will be more and even bigger raids before the second front

Dead Canadian at Dieppe

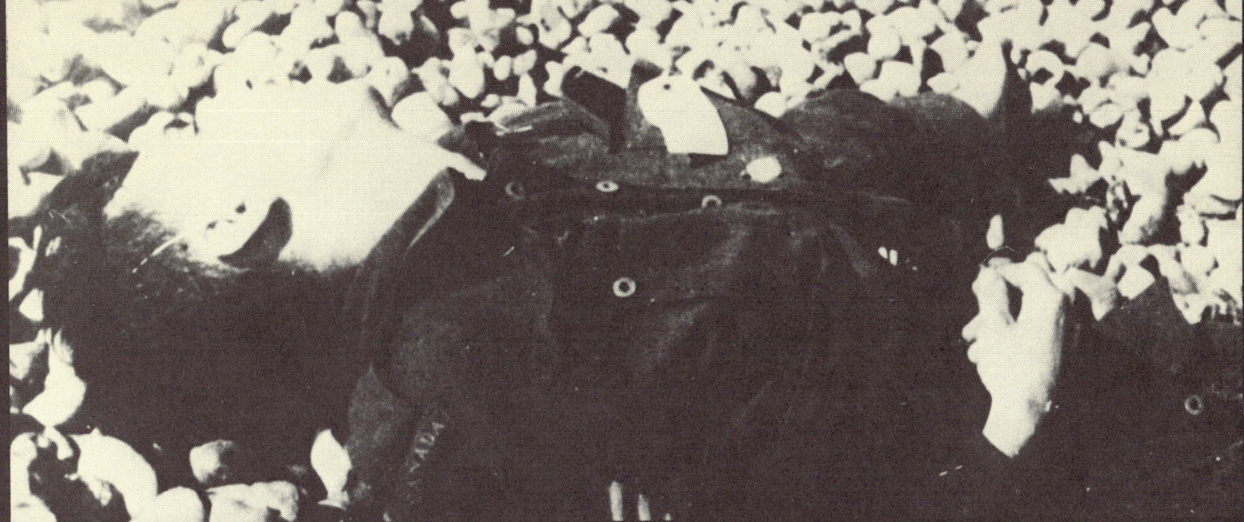

Back at Dieppe, the fighting petered out around 13:00. . . and the Germans emerged to collect the surrendering troops and to take care of the dead and wounded.

Germans round up prisoners

German soldier after the battle

German soldiers looking for survivors of the raid

German soldiers view the beach at Pourville

Canadians surrendering

Canadian and Royal Navy survivors who had tried to swim to freedom were rounded up and taken prisoner.

Rounding up Canadians and Royal Navy men who had tried to swim out to their ships

German anti-tank gun in cliff cave at Dieppe

German soldiers on the west headland at Dieppe

The victorious defenders inspected damage to their defences and dealt with the wounded—their own . . .

German wounded at Dieppe

. . .and ours.

Germans attending to Canadian wounded

Wasted lives and equipment on the beach at Dieppe

Germans celebrate their victory on the beach

Even in the midst of horror, there were moments of celebration.

"The German soldier flipped the top off three more bottles of beer and handed one to myself and one to the fellow on the ground. So I had a drink or two of this beer and I was standing there and I thought, this is ridiculous..."

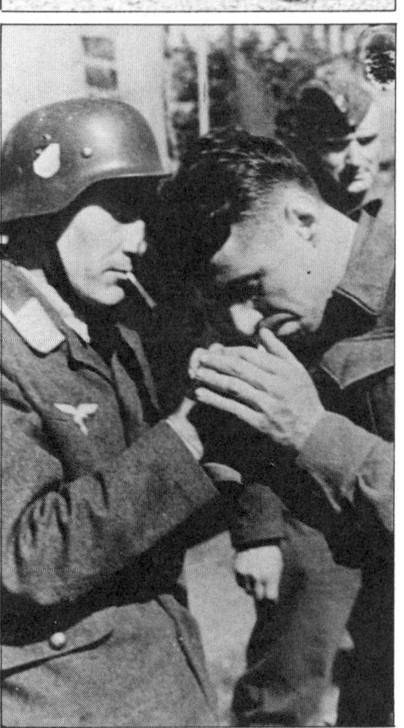

A German and his prisoner ... a Canadian Lieutenant

"Here we were a couple of hours ago, shooting at one another, to kill. And here we are now, just a couple of soldiers, standing having a beer together."

The victor

German soldiers began to gather the bodies that littered the beach.

"What especially impressed me was a Canadian or an Englishman—I don't know which—sitting in an armoured scout car, burned to the bone. His gleaming bones sat there in the scout car as if he wanted to drive on further."

Germans collect charred bodies of Canadian dead

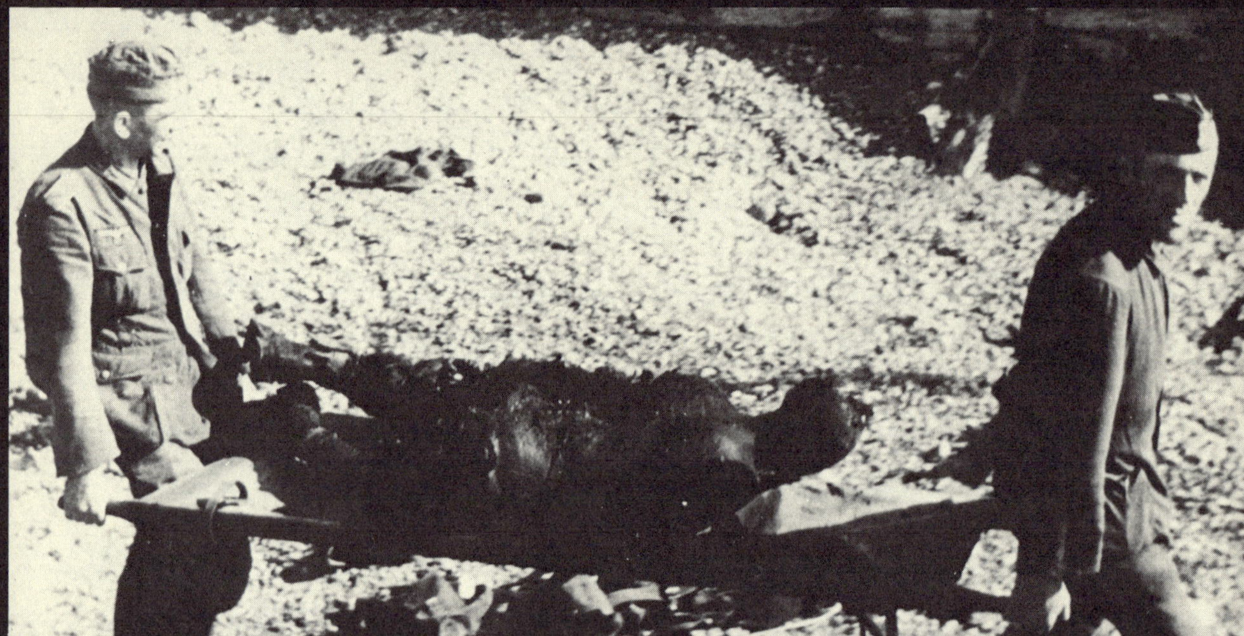

"It was not a pretty picture. . .it really wasn't."

Germans collecting Canadian dead

A local canoe brings in a drowned Canadian

Abandoned scout car at Dieppe

"The dead on the beach... I've never seen such obscenities before...."

"There were pieces of human beings littering the beach. There were headless bodies, there were legs, there were arms. And they looked inhuman. I had no shoes and there were shoes lying around. With feet in them."

Mangled bodies in a stranded landing craft

“War is nothing but a waste.”

Devastation at Dieppe

Every tank landed had to be sacrificed.

"We knew—once we saw just where our objectives lay—we knew that they would never get us back to England. It was just. . .tough luck, fellows."

Victorious Germans and an abandoned Canadian tank at Dieppe

Germans had not seen the new Churchill tank before

The German army naturally showed keen interest in the Allied vehicles and craft left behind.

Sepp Dietrich, Commander of Adolph Hitler SS Division inspects captured tanks

Albert Speer inspects captured tanks

Field-Marshal von Rundstedt viewing the aftermath of the Dieppe raid

Gen. Adolph Gallandt, head of Luftwaffe fighter aircraft, inspects landing craft

"Hitler had told his soldiers that the men who hold the Channel ports command Europe . . ."

". . .and this put every German soldier on his mettle. It gave him pride, it gave him that *esprit de corps* which we were possibly lacking as we were only just recovering from the humiliation of Dunkirk. We were only learning to be soldiers all over again."

Lord Lovat,
No. 4 Commando

Abandoned tanks on the beach with the Chateau in the background

German soldiers relax at the Chateau on the west headland, Dieppe, 1942 (Emil Kilgast on the left)

"Fear? The Canadians weren't shooting peas, you know. We were getting the same thing up here that they were down there!"

Emil Kilgast's post was near the château on the west headland.

"I had only been a soldier for a few months. For me, it was a baptism of fire."

Emil Kilgast today

And then the clean-up began in town . . .

Dieppe streets showed the intensity of shelling during the raid

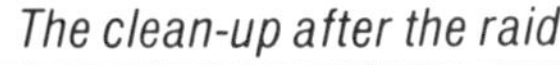

The clean-up after the raid

. . .while almost 2,000 Allied prisoners marched away.

Canadians taken prisoner at Pourville

French nursing sisters care for the wounded prisoners at the hospital in Dieppe

The more seriously wounded among the prisoners were tended by German medics and French nursing sisters.

Wounded prisoners at Dieppe

Germans looking after wounded Canadians

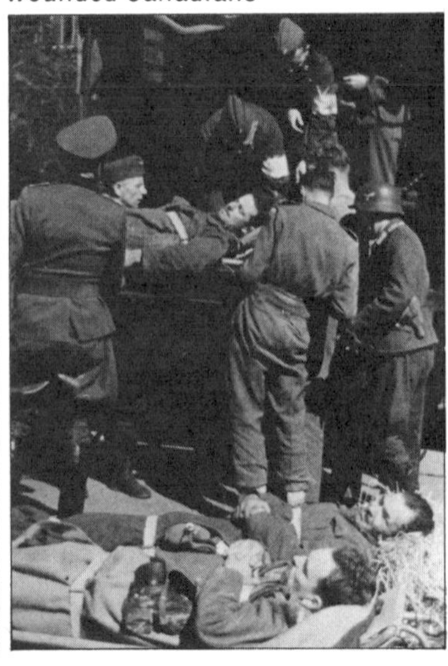

German medical corps attending to wounded Canadians

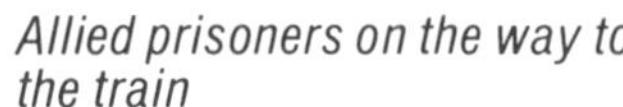

Allied prisoners on the way to the train

The rest were marched several kilometres to catch the trains that would take them to prison camp in Germany.

Now was the time to wonder: what went wrong?

"I think if you're going to sacrifice a division, you've got to be prepared to put in a capital ship—a six-inch cruiser, something like that. And this they didn't do."

"Well, the operation as a whole, I think, should never have been attempted. The beaches, the way they were obviously covered by machine-gun fire from the cliffs on either side. . .they were a complete death-trap."

"If the Canadian forces on that occasion had had some battle experience—if they'd been blooded—I think the results would have been a great deal different."

"Coming in raw like that, when you know that all of a sudden it's for real instead of just practising and training. . .if things go wrong we didn't seem to be able to improvise."

Canadian P.O.W.'s at Pourville

Allied prisoners were marched through Dieppe

Canadian P.O.W.'s

"People excused Dieppe by saying, 'Well, we learned by our mistakes.' But we didn't need to make the mistakes we made at Dieppe. Surely they should have had a better concept of the kind of plan they should have had without having to have a Dieppe disaster."

"They didn't have the experience of an operation that size. Nobody had any experience. So errors were committed and were to be expected. Except that it was a costly error."

"It was useless. It was unnecessary and I don't feel that my sacrifice and the sacrifice of the men who were killed accomplished anything."

"Without Dieppe we couldn't have had the invasion. Without the invasion we couldn't have won the war."

"Eight or ten hours and it was all over. And that was *my* war."

"We were sold out. Somewhere along the line, we'd been sold down the river."

Resting Allied prisoners

Envermeu was a collecting point for Canadian prisoners. It was also where M. and Mme. Jean Dupuis were married that day.

M. and Mme. Dupuis on August 19, 1942

Canadian P.O.W.'s resting at Envermeu on the way to the trains

Church at Envermeu, near Dieppe, where some prisoners were locked up for the night

"Well, I was a young bride and I was so happy that day. We took a walk and were very surprised to meet these prisoners. At first we thought it was the invasion—the end of the war."

"It is the custom in Normandy to go on a walk after a wedding, with the two families and the wedding guests. It was a beautiful day and we started walking towards Dieppe."

"We were being marched up the road, and my feet were cut to ribbons. . .and we spotted this wedding party coming towards us."

M. and Mme. Dupuis in 1978

"Here, honey, have a good time on us!"

"The guys were digging in their pockets for money, and throwing it at the bride and groom."

"We picked up one of the coins and made it our wedding piece. We had it engraved with our wedding date, which is the same day we ran into the Canadian prisoners."

The Dupuis wedding coin, an English penny, thrown to them by a Canadian P.O.W.

Dupuis wedding party—end of the day, August 19, 1942. One of the men has picked up a Canadian helmet

Canadian P.O.W.'s on the way to the train

Mme. Yvette Robillard (on the right) whose husband (standing at the back) gave the shoes to Stanley Darch

Stanley Darch, who was given a pair of shoes by one of the Dupuis wedding party

Stan Darch of the R.H.L.I. was given a pair of shoes for his bleeding feet.

"My husband saw that one of the Canadian soldiers had bare feet. My husband took off his own shoes and threw them to the Canadian."

"They were a beautiful brown pair of shoes—patent leather. And I sat on the curb and pulled them on and just as I was getting up this German came along behind me and gave me a boot in the backside for sitting down and taking so long."

"The Germans arrested my husband, but he only did this as a humanitarian gesture. They understood, and soon afterwards my husband was returned."

The station at Envermeu from which Canadian P.O.W.'s left for German prison camps

Bravery was rewarded. Decorations were won by German soldiers . . .

German soldiers with Iron Crosses won at Dieppe

. . .and by French commandos.

Free French commandos being decorated in London for valour at Dieppe

Canadian officers holding banner presented by the French P.O.W.'s who were returned to their homes after the Dieppe raid

John Foote today

Maj. John Foote, the R.H.L.I. chaplain, won the Victoria Cross.

Padre Foote was given a chance to be evacuated from the beach, but refused to leave his men. He helped care for and comfort the R.H.L.I. wounded at Dieppe under heavy fire, and remained with his men in a German prison camp throughout the rest of the war.

"My job was to be with the men. Religion is a part of life, to me, and if you're going to have a chaplain service in the army, it doesn't look very good for the chaplain to stay at home."

"The medical officer and myself had gone up to the hospital and were working along with the others to look after the wounded when I was tapped on the shoulder by a German officer and taken away. I was taken to one room for interrogation and Captain Claire was taken to another. After an hour we came out and the two German officers joined us. And the one said to the other, 'Well, this is certainly the army. Out of all the people who were at Dieppe, we chose at random two people who know nothing about the military situation. One is the chaplain and the other is a medical officer!' "

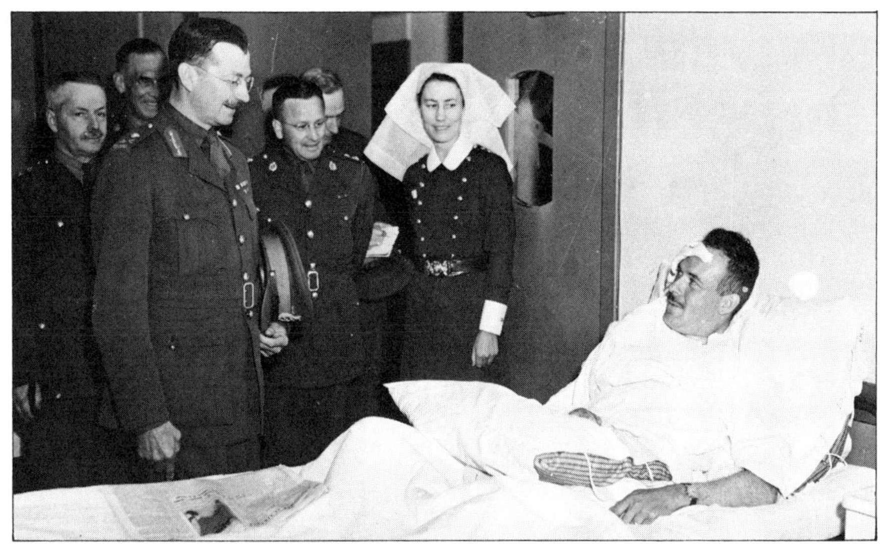

Dollard Menard in hospital after the raid

Dollard Menard, of the F.M.R., was the only battalion commander to fight on the beaches and also get safely back to England.

"It's quite normal to be hit once. But when you're hit twice you feel quite safe because this is abnormal. So after I'd been hit twice I said, 'Well, at least I'm scot-free now.' But then I got hit the third time. And that never happens. So I started to blame the teachers who had taught me the statistics of casualties, and I started to get a bit mad at them. But when I was hit the fourth time, I really decided the book should be thrown away because there was nothing good in it. And by the time I was hit the fifth time, I didn't believe much in anything."

Those who survived Dieppe would never forget it . . . .

"It was the biggest thing in *my* life. . ."

"I grew up that day—from a boy—to know what the world was all about."

"I came to the conclusion that wars should all be fought by men over fifty. That would save young people for better things."

Propaganda pictures hardly gave the true picture of the state of things in the hospitals.

"I shall never forget walking into that ward. The suffering was incredible. Every bed was occupied and the air was full of groans and pathetic hoarse whispers. The men's faces were all covered with black spots from the shell blasts. A hefty Canadian was in agony. When the sheet was pulled back I noticed that the whole of his body was split open from chin to groin—a jagged, red, wide wound, so terrible that it seemed as if his very insides were coming out. It was a terrible sight and a traumatic experience. I was only twenty-two years old and although we had experienced the bombs in London this was our first sight of badly wounded casualties. I felt infinite pity for this Canadian and aghast at the barbaric cruelty of war. I heard that he had died in the night and I was very sad. I had felt that he was my personal patient, although I had done so little for him. I like to think that he had got as far as the operating theatre in spite of the queues, and that they had done what they could for him, but I never knew."

. . . and once they recovered from the wounds and shocks of their first battle, their regiments would be rebuilt and go on to fight bravely and successfully in the rest of the war.

Hospitalized Canadian who made it back

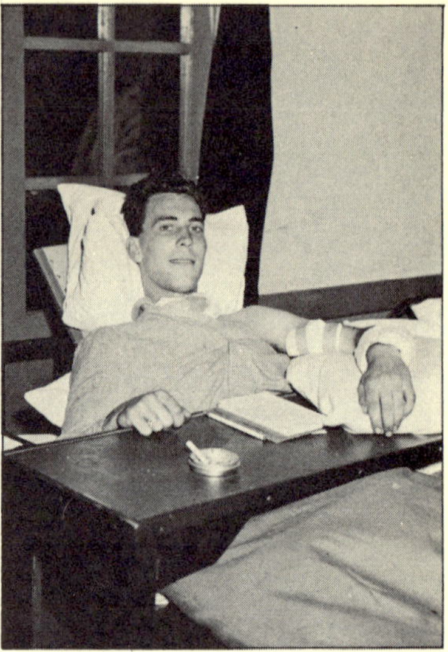

Canadian survivors back in camp in England

Pte. Leo DeLaurier and Pte. Robert Baker of the Essex Scottish Regiment

One of the wounded

War correspondent interviewing a wounded soldier

Sorting through the equipment of those who did not return safely

Those who died would always be remembered.

"I still see them in my mind, and I'm very sorry for them. I think. . .I could well have been one of them. But that's not important."

"Also, you know you're growing older. . .but they didn't have the chance to grow older."

Led. by Maj. Gen. Roberts, Gen. McNaughton and Gen. Crerar, Canadian officers attend funeral of those who died of wounds received at Dieppe

Burial of Canadians who died of wounds received at Dieppe—Brookwood Cemetery, England, August, 1942

Burial of Canadians who died of wounds received at Dieppe—Brookwood Cemetery, England, August, 1942

For some, the battle of Dieppe would ultimately bring great joy....

The Allies had asked the French civilians around Dieppe to stay out of the fighting. Ironically, as a reward to the people of Dieppe for staying neutral, Hitler freed 1,400 French prisoners of war and sent them home to their families.

Official reception party for the return of French P.O.W.'s to Dieppe

French P.O.W.'s in German prison camp

French P.O.W.'s return to Dieppe

Field-Marshal von Rundstedt and German officers examining a copy of the Allied battle plan, captured at Dieppe

For many Canadian P.O.W.'s, there was a shaming experience....

Two copies of the Allied battle plan, in full detail, were taken ashore during the raid. In the confusion of the evacuation, one copy fell into enemy hands. Thus the Germans discovered that Canadian soldiers, contrary to the Geneva Convention, had been ordered to tie the hands of any Germans taken prisoner during the battle.

In retaliation Hitler ordered guards at German prison camps to manacle Canadian prisoners of war every day for months.

"We shouldn't have tied our prisoners up in the first place. But we had limited men to look after those people. And at the time we certainly didn't do it to be vicious or mean. But when the Germans tied *us* up, then the thought strikes you—well, this is certainly a terrible thing to do to a soldier. I mean, how could I be punished for carrying out my orders?"

Manacled Canadian P.O.W.

Sections of Mulberry Harbour

Lord Louis Mountbatten

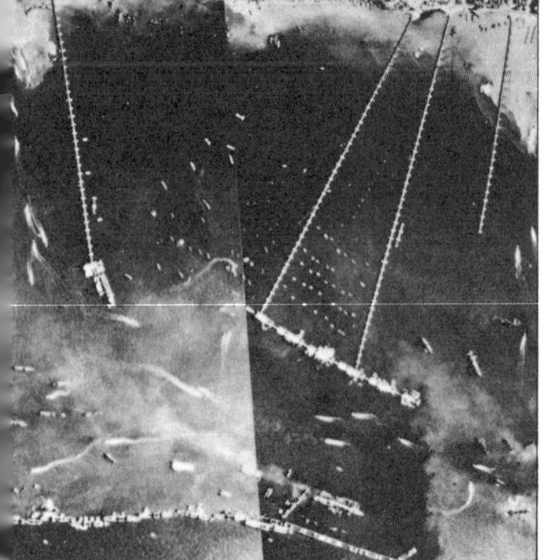

"The Duke of Wellington said that the Battle of Waterloo was won on the playing fields of Eton, and I say that the Battle of Normandy was won on the beaches of Dieppe." —Lord Louis Mountbatten

"The total lesson learned from Dieppe was unquestionably that you cannot in fact capture a port by frontal assault without having such heavy bombardment and bombing as to destroy the port facilities for which you are trying to capture it."

"So we learned that we must land across open beaches. . .and because the weather is so bad in the Channel, we certainly, within three or four days, would have been unable to continue to supply across these beaches. For the Normandy invasion, we therefore developed a portable prefabricated harbour known as Mulberry. It was much scoffed at at the time, but it saved the invasion. And this would not have had backing unless there'd been the experience of Dieppe to prove that it was necessary."

Men of the 9th Infantry Brigade are landed at Bernieres beachhead by the Royal Canadian Navy, June, 1944—D-Day

The invasion, when it finally came, took Canadians back to Dieppe for the first time since the raid. . .and this time, as the victors.

After the war, they have kept going back to Dieppe. . .to honour their dead comrades.

Prime Minister Mackenzie King at commemorative ceremony at Puys, 1946

Canadian troops return to Dieppe during the liberation of France, 1944

The ceremony at Puys, 1946

Corp. Leo Leckie and wife

A Canadian prisoner of war and his wartime memories. . . .

Leo Leckie of the Queen's Own Cameron Highlanders was among those eventually released from a German prison camp and returned safely to his family. He brought with him the drawings and cartoons he had collected over the three years he had spent as a P.O.W. They remain as an individualistic retelling of the story of Dieppe.

Corp. Leo Leckie's scrapbook which he kept while in the prison camp

19 AUG
DIEPPE
1942
POUMAINE 43
11

WHERE I LANDED
12

DIEPPE
44 POUMAINE
13

NIP GOES TO WAR!!
IDEA
?
WAR WE NEED YOU!
OUTFIT
120
MARCH-HALT.
CLIFF-SCALE
FURLOUGH
123
INVASION
FRONT LINES
118
TRY-ON
SQUARE BASH
121
Commando Training
CLIFF-SCALE
FURLOUGH
SALE
124
Soup-up!!
119
DRAFT
B.H.Q. GUARD!
122
A.W.L.
BLACK-OUT!!
114
"BREW-UP"

75

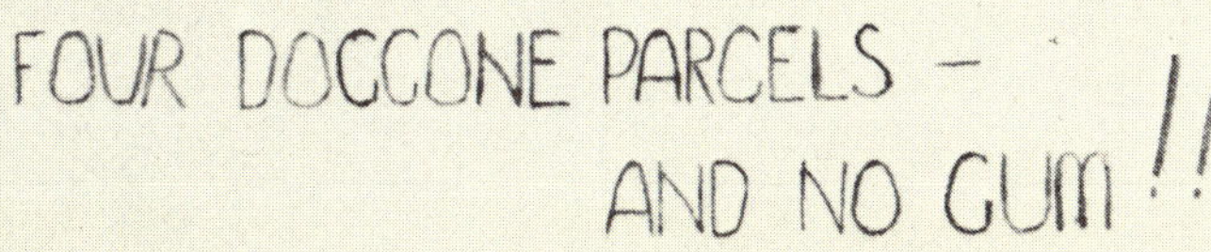

BEST WISHES
D. QUENBY
STANMORE
MIDDLESEX
ENGLAND

—BUT I TOLD YOU IT WAS TEN METRES FURTHER, THEY COME UP

DAWN
AND
DIEPPE

Canadian and German veterans visiting Dieppe cemetery, 1978

Those who fought at Dieppe keep coming back. . .in person, and in memory.

"I go every year, but after all this time, what do we pray for? There's nobody there, there's nothing. We just pray to an empty tomb. So what did we gain? Nothing."

"When I see these graves—kids, twenty. . .twenty-one—it breaks my heart. There was no need for it. No need for it."

"It was an awful waste. . .and to see them go leaves an awful memory."

"My memory says this did happen. My conscience says 'twere better it had not happened. Gradually, memory yields to the dictates of conscience."

—Friedrich Nietzsche

Veterans and Canadian headstones in Dieppe cemetery

"It had to be done. . .but the sacrifice, it was awful."

Why was the raid mounted in the first place?

—Canadian soldiers and their families were pressing to get our troops out of British training camps and into action.

—Americans and Russians were demanding that a second front be opened in Europe.

—Allied military leaders believed that without a full-scale trial, a major invasion of Europe would never succeed.

—Once Combined Operations existed as a planning unit specializing in amphibious assaults, it was inevitable that such a plan would be tried out.

Why was the raid such a disaster?

—The planning was faulty: too detailed and inflexible, and based on insufficient intelligence of German defences at Dieppe.

—There was insufficient support from the navy and air force; although heavy bombing (which General Roberts agreed to have cancelled), would have caused many civilian deaths as well as possibly destroying the harbour facilities that made Dieppe of value, and although it would have been risky to have a battleship operating in the restricted waters of the Channel, without these added armaments the raid was bound to fail.

—The Canadians were well trained but they lacked battle experience and consequently could not overcome the many inadequacies of the planning.

What did it accomplish?

—The lessons learned were successfully applied on D-Day in the invasion of France in 1944—especially the need to avoid the heavily defended ports and land on open beaches, which meant having the mobile prefabricated harbours code-named Mulberry.

Was it all worth it?

"Our two former enemies are the richest nations in the world and our late allies are all squabbling like mad. Where did it get us? Nowhere."

"The important thing to me is that what was learned at Dieppe saved an awful lot of lives on D-Day. We paid a terrible price. . .but it wasn't all for nothing."

Mrs. Mary Barrow in Brookwood Cemetery

"The same as any mother who has given birth to sons to have them murdered by the whims of stupid politicians. . .I hate war."

"Life, to be sure, is nothing much to lose. But young men think it is. . .and we were young."

Index

Further Reading

There is a considerable literature on Dieppe, some of it unreliable. For an excellent analysis see Col. C.P. Stacey's *Six Years of War,* vol. I (p. 310-412). A popular book, inaccurate in some details but giving a very good sense of what it was all about, is Terence Robertson's *The Shame and the Glory.* A personal view from a sergeant in the F.M.R.'s who escaped from the prison train and later went back into France for M.I. 9 is offered in *The Man Who Went Back* by Lucian Dumais. John Mellors' *Forgotten Heroes* contains accounts of P.O.W. life. A good political background and account can be found in Jacques Mordal's *Dieppe—Dawn of Decision,* translated from the French. In French, see *Operation Jubilee* by Claude-Paul Coutoure and *Le Jubilé des Canadians* by Raymond Rudler. Lord Lovat's *March Past* gives a perceptive look at the British No. 4 Commando operation (p. 222-279). Essential for the tactical situation on the ground or for anyone visiting Dieppe is *After the Battle* (Number 5, Editor Winston G. Ramsey), a meticulously researched and condensed account of the fighting.

Credits

Photographs

Bundesarchiv Koblenz: 10-11, 15-19, 33, 41, 45, 47 upper, 61, 63, 86, 106 left, 108, 124 upper, 126 lower, 137-138, 139 lower, 140, 141 upper and lower right, 143, 147, 148 centre, 149-150, 151 upper and centre, 152-153, 154 lower left, 156-157, 158 centre, 159 lower, 160 lower, 162, 170-172; **City of Toronto Archives, James Collection:** 20 lower, 21 upper; ***The Hamilton Spectator:*** 136; **Kenneth Hyde:** 173; **Imperial War Museum:** 12, 29, 30 upper and lower right, 33 upper left, 32, 43, 51, 65, 71 lower left, 75 lower, 79 left, 89, 91, 106 right, 110, 111 right, 114 upper, 118 lower, 121 lower, 125 upper, 130-133, 134 lower, 135 centre and lower; **Terence Macartney-Filgate:** 74, 86 upper right, 92 upper, 109, 113, 115 lower right, 123, 130 upper left, 151 lower, 164, 174 upper right, 184-185, 188; **Gilbert A. Milne, Toronto:** 175; **Public Archives Canada:** 21 lower, 22-23, 25 lower, 30 lower right, 31 upper right, 34-37, 40, 44, 46, 48, 50, 65 lower, 66 upper, 78, 79 right, 81, 111 left, 114 lower, 118 upper, 121 centre, 124, 134 upper and centre, 135 upper, 165-166, 167 centre and lower, 168-169, 174 lower, centre and upper left, 175; **Studio Goron:** 122; ***The Toronto Star:*** 20.

Illustrations

Gordon Wilson: 68-69, 71, 73, 84-85, 94-95, 102-104, 107, 112-113, 116-117, 125-127, 129, (photographs of paintings by Paul Till); **Leo Leckie's scrapbook** on pp. 178-183 photographed by Paul Till; **Map on p. 111: permission granted by Canadian Government Publishing Centre.**

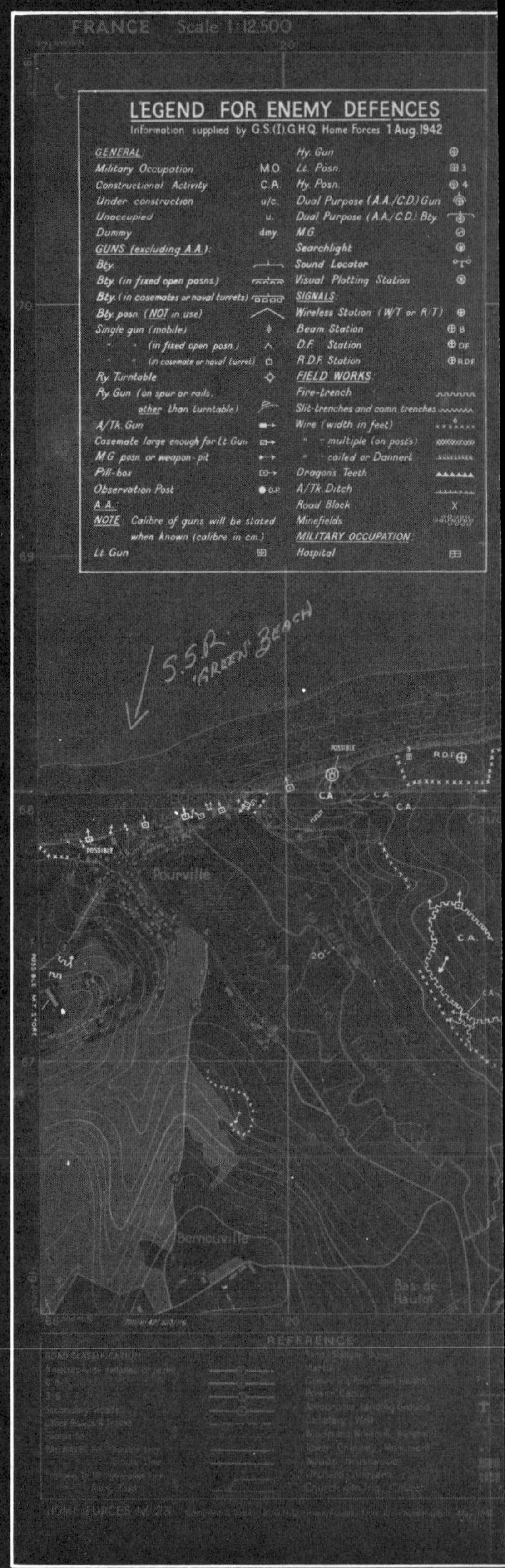

Each regiment in the Dieppe raid was issued this operational planning map, marking enemy gun emplacements, and barbed wire barriers as pinpointed by aerial photographs and intelligence reports.

Unfortunately, the map showed only a fraction of the armaments and defenses that would create such chaos during the landing.

This copy of the top secret map was kept, against orders, by one of the regimental adjutants, a sorrowful souvenir of a massive assault that was doomed from the start.